Political Cyberbullying

Political Cyberbullying

PERPETRATORS AND TARGETS OF A NEW DIGITAL AGGRESSION

Sheri Bauman

An Imprint of ABC-CLIO, LLC
Santa Barbara, California • Denver, Colorado

Library of Congress Cataloging in Publication Control Number: 2019040324

ISBN: 978-1-4408-6687-6 (print)
      978-1-4408-6688-3 (ebook)

24 23 22 21 20   1 2 3 4 5

This book is also available as an eBook.

Praeger
An Imprint of ABC-CLIO, LLC

ABC-CLIO, LLC
147 Castilian Drive
Santa Barbara, California 93117
www.abc-clio.com

This book is printed on acid-free paper (∞)

Manufactured in the United States of America

To my husband Bob, for his unfailing love and support

Contents

Acknowledgments

I would like to first thank all the people who shared their personal stories of digital aggression and allowed me to use them in this book. Many of these stories were painful to talk about, and I am grateful that I was trusted to hear them and hope that I am seen as having done so with compassion. My former student, Melissa Burstein, was an invaluable assistant in getting the final form of the book ready, and I sincerely appreciate her help. I thank my friend Dr. Syd Arkowitz, a psychoanalyst, for her thoughts on Chapter 4, "Online Disinhibition Effect." My husband, Bob, patiently read the drafts of each chapter and caught typos and gave useful feedback. And, finally, I appreciate Debbie Carvalko at Praeger who gave me the opportunity to write and publish this book.

1

Introduction

I planned to begin this book with a dramatic example of digital aggression, so I have been hypervigilant about relevant sensational news and activity on social media. Each time I learned of a new event, I would think, "That's it. That's such an egregious example, nothing will be more extraordinary—my search is over." And then the next incident would appear, and the next. In fact, dramatic incidents abound, but I fear the shock value has diminished. Perhaps I have become cynical, jaded, desensitized. Since the campaign leading up to the American presidential election in 2016, it seems the tempo and boldness of digital incivility and aggression have increased. This book aims to understand this phenomenon.

An example—far from the worst—of the sort of interactions that are all too common commonplace online—is the experience of Mara Reinstein (2019), a movie critic who publishes her reviews on *US Weekly* and MaraMovies.com. Her reviews are also linked to popular movie rating sites such as Rotten Tomatoes. In January 2019, she published a review of *Aquaman*, which was less than favorable (I confess I haven't seen it, so I have no opinion on the merit of the film). A movie critic's reviews are clearly and obviously opinion pieces, presenting a particular point of view. Therefore, some readers will disagree. But the barrage of hateful and threatening messages she received is chilling: *"Hey what pathetic looser [sic] you are. I will kill your mom, dad and friends Bcoz I want [you] to regret for what you did. I have your address and details about your family members." "Wait don't take this as a joke, next time if your parents die in a shooting or bombing . . . don't [say] I didn't warn you." "I hope U just die."* I haven't included the more vulgar and sexually graphic comments, but I suspect you get the idea. How is it that disagreeing with a movie review leads to death threats? What's more, when Reinstein reported these messages to Instagram, it did not remove them because they apparently were not in violation of community guidelines. Facebook and Twitter were also used to harass her, including this: "btw your last name sounds Jewish so no surprise you are such an ignorant person hope another Holocaust happens." Reinstein observed that there is a gendered nature to these attacks, with many offensive terms used and comments about her appearance and anatomy being frequent.

Lest anyone doubt the power of social media, keep in mind that a tweet on August 5, 2018, by the Canadian ambassador to Saudi Arabia resulted in a diplomatic furor that caused the Canadian envoy to be barred from returning to Saudi Arabia, the Saudi ambassador to Canada to be recalled, and new trade restrictions to be implemented. Also in August 2018, a post on an Oklahoma school's parents' Facebook page that was perceived to be a threat of violence toward a student caused schools to be closed for several days and of course was widely reported on news and social media sites. In that same month, a Black female member of the Vermont state legislature withdrew her candidacy for reelection (Lewis, 2018). In her announcement, she stated, "Political discourse, and in particular within the sphere of social media has been divisive, inflammatory, and at times, even dangerous." Among the threats she had received was this one: Max Misch of Bennington posted on Twitter last week a cartoon caricature of a black person, with the caption, "S---, I be representin dem white m---f--- of Bennington, gnome sayin?" The local newspaper, *The Banner*, dashed certain of Misch's words for publication (Carson, 2016). Misch was not charged for his racial harassment of Kiah Morris, as the attorney general found that the hate speech in which Misch engaged was protected by the First Amendment. However, in February 2019, he was arrested for owning the type of high-capacity gun magazine that was outlawed in Vermont (Keays, 2019). Although the possession of this equipment was not directly related to his threats against Kiah Morris and her family, it gives one pause to know that he had access to such lethal weapons, while continuing to espouse White supremacist and anti-Semitic rhetoric.

In this chapter, I provide background information that sets the stage for the rest of the book. I provide data on the extent to which our world has become a digital one and offer my views on the terminology used to describe the negative online content to which we are exposed. I look at the variety of platforms the internet provides for expressing one's views and then give an overview of how the First Amendment affects efforts to restrict harmful content. Finally, I consider the research that has been done to date to ensure readers are familiar with the scholarly literature on the topic.

Chapter 2 focuses on various theories of aggression and evaluates those theories' potential as explanations for online hostility and cyberaggression. One of those theories, the *online disinhibition effect*, will be covered in detail in Chapter 4. In Chapter 3, I discuss the behavior of high-status, high-visibility persons, from celebrities to statespersons, and consider how those role models affect the tenor of online material. Digital personas, or the personalities revealed online, are the subject of Chapter 5. In Chapter 6, I explore the behavior and motivation of *trolls*, those who purposely cause shock and distress in the digital environment. I then examine the topics of revenge porn/slut shaming and dating sites in Chapter 7. Chapter 8 will conclude with a discussion of strategies to cope with digital aggression, so that we can derive the many benefits of the digital universe while protecting ourselves from harm. Throughout the book, in each chapter, I include stories of people who have been the targets of digital aggression so that the data and theories have a human face. I call them simply "Stories" and invite readers to reflect on how these examples of cyberbullying are related to the political world.

BACKGROUND

America is clearly a digitally saturated society. Seventy-seven percent of Americans have a smartphone (and 95% have some type of mobile phone) (Pew Research Center, 2018); only 35% of Americans had smartphones in 2011. Perhaps as a consequence of the ubiquitous access, 67% of adults and 90% of young adults engage with social media (Smyth, 2016). An increasing portion of Americans access news online (43% compared to 50% whose source is television, 25% who listen to news on radio, and 18% who read a print newspaper) (Gottfried & Shearer, 2017); updated data suggest as many as 93% of American adults get at least some news reports online. Only 11% of Americans chose not to use the internet in 2018 compared to 48% in 2000 (Anderson, Perrin, & Jiang, 2018); there is no reason to believe the trend toward increased digital connectivity will not continue.

Americans of all ages conduct much of their lives digitally. The issue that concerns us here is the nature of digital interactions and the unkind, uncivil, and sometimes threatening treatment of others that is too readily observable in this environment. A 2017 report (Duggan, 2017) found that 66% of Americans had witnessed some form of online abuse or aggression, and 41% had a personal experience of such behavior. The kinds of behavior that witnesses report include name-calling, deliberate embarrassment, threatening, sexual harassment, and so on. These data point to the magnitude of the problem of digital aggression. The severity of the problem is demonstrated by the 18% of those who experienced severe victimization, including threats, ongoing harassment, and stalking. Political views were the most common reason people believed they were targeted (14%), with race, gender, and physical appearance just below 10%. The majority of survey respondents (62%) indicated online harassment was a major problem, which is the raison d'etre for this book.

Consequences of Digital Aggression

Research on cyberbullying has focused primarily on children and adolescents. The most consistent findings are that involvement in cyberbullying is associated with higher levels of depression and anxiety, suicidal behaviors, and somatic symptoms (headaches, stomach distress, sleep disturbances) (Meter & Bauman, 2018). In addition, some researchers have found elevated rates of delinquency and substance abuse among cyberbullies (Ybarra & Mitchell, 2007). Overall, cyberbullying has been found to result in diminished quality of life and well-being for adolescents (Davison & Stein, 2014).

Privitera and Campbell (2009) cited studies that reported harmful consequences of workplace cyber bullying, including low morale, decreased job satisfaction, disruption of relationships, increased absenteeism, and high rates of employee turnover, and Sansone and Sansone (2015) found similar negative outcomes, including fatigue, depression, anxiety, physical problems, and even suicide. In one of the few studies of workplace cyberbullying, Coyne et al. (2017) found that being exposed to cyberbullying had a greater negative impact on job satisfaction than did offline bullying.

On a broader societal level, consider the events of December 5, 2018, when the stock market lost 799 points in one day, which several financial analysts believed to be due, in part, to a tweet in which President Trump called himself "Tariff Man." The worldwide ramifications of such volatility are well known, so the effect of a single tweet can be global. In another example, Milo Yiannopoulos, a conservative provocateur, sent a text message to journalists saying, "I can't wait for the vigilante squads to start gunning journalists down on sight." The journalists publicized this comment when, several days later, there was a fatal shooting of journalists at the *Capital Gazette* newspaper in Annapolis, Maryland. Twitter erupted with condemnation of Yiannopoulos. In a Facebook post, he defended himself, and claimed the comment was a "private joke" or an "offhand troll," and blamed the journalists who publicized the comment. A popular comedian whose selection as the host of the 2019 Academy Awards was initially lauded resigned from that job because of criticism of tweets from several years earlier that were construed to be insensitive to the LGBT community. Although Kevin Hart apologized (on Instagram), he ultimately chose to step down and announced that decision on Twitter. The influence of social media in contemporary American society is difficult to exaggerate.

To date, no research that identified effects of cyberbullying in the general adult population has been published. The following anecdotes are illustrations of the kinds of experiences and aftermaths of specific incidents.

Some Examples

It is easy to frame the toxic component of the digital world as a function of the political divisions that afflict the nation. While it is certainly the case that the contentious political discourse has contributed to the erosion of civility online (more on this later), it is an oversimplification to characterize all the aggression as politically motivated. For example, I subscribe to a listserv for professors and graduate students in my field. In addition to the useful information and announcements circulated on this list, there are occasional incidents of digital aggression. One such incident occurred in April 2018, when a listmember posted the words to a Christian hymn in honor of Easter. Another member praised the contribution. However, others on the list felt that the academic focus of the listserv precluded such religious expressions, and felt it was exclusionary since not all members of the list are Christian. The post soon involved a larger conversation of religious bias, with more pointed—some might say inflammatory—remarks directed at individual members who were seen by some to be insensitive or biased.

I was the target of a more deliberate and potentially damaging cyberattack in the early 2000s; e-mail was the weapon. I participated in an online study group for a licensing exam (I was completing my PhD in counseling psychology), and someone who was doing an internship in a place I had once lived joined the group. I requested that person e-mail me directly, and we corresponded briefly about common friends, favorite restaurants, and so on. A few months later, I received an e-mail from her saying she was going to report me to my university and state licensing board to ensure I never got credentials as a psychologist. I had no idea what she was talking about. It turns out that someone had impersonated me, and e-mailed this person and several others with graphic, vulgar, unwanted sexual messages. I eventually was able to contact the owner of the listserv, who then tracked down the computer (using the IP address) from which these despicable e-mails were sent, but the person whose computer was identified claimed he was on vacation during that time period and that a house guest must have sent them as a practical joke. Regardless of the veracity of that explanation, the list owner did damage control and my graduation and licensure were not affected. This appeared to be a random targeting and demonstrates how being online can make anyone vulnerable to those with nefarious intentions.

Politically Tinged Cyberaggression

We hear much about the vast chasm that divides the political spectrum in the United States, and we know that digital aggression comes from both positions. However, it does seem that politically tinged aggression easily becomes more extreme. I will discuss the practice of trolling in more detail in Chapter 5, but other forms of aggression also have a political purpose.

One example revolves around a case of mis-identification. During the 2017 Charlottesville march by White supremacists, someone who viewed a video of the event mis-identified Kyle Quinn (a professor from Arkansas) as a White supremacist taking part in the march. The individual in the video was actually a man named Andrew Dodson (who self-identified later). However, Quinn quickly became the target of vulgar and threatening e-mails and posts on Twitter, Instagram, and Facebook; some of the posts included identifying information such as his home address, which was very frightening for him and his family. This attack is an example of the digital version of mob mentality, with people joining in the fray without bothering to verify information.

In another example Aaron Scholossberg, an attorney in New York City, one of the most diverse places in the country, loudly berated Spanish-speaking staff and customers at a Manhattan restaurant for speaking that language to each other and Spanish-speaking patrons. His behavior was boorish and would once have been handled by the restaurant. He might have been asked to leave, denied service, and so on. If his belligerence persisted, perhaps police would be called for assistance in removing him from the premises. However, this rant occurred in 2018—so another patron at the restaurant video-recorded the incident and posted it online, where it "went viral." The man then lost his job, received threats, and was chastised in explicit terms on various social media.

From the other side of the political spectrum comes Adam Smith, a Tucson, Arizona, businessman who was angry that the Chick-fil-A CEO had made public statements demeaning LGBT+ persons. In response, Smith harangued an employee of the local franchise, recorded his diatribe, and the posted it online. Again, it was widely disseminated, and in this case, Smith also lost his job (his employer did not appreciate the video) and received death and other threats against himself and his family to the point that he took his family out of the country for several years.

A final example is perhaps the highest-profile incident in recent years. Christine Blasey Ford accused Brett Kavanaugh, a nominee for a seat on the U.S. Supreme Court, of sexual assault when both were in high school, and she testified before Congress about the incident. Once her name was publicized, the cyberattacks began—which included hate e-mail, death threats, and *doxing* (publicizing her address on Twitter) (Durkin, 2018; Gardner, 2018). The vehemence and the vulgarity of the threats, which included threats to her family members, forced Ford into hiding, disrupting her life. In this case, Trump weighed in on Twitter, implying that since she did not report the incident at the time (when she was 15 years old), it must not be true. Supporters of Ford raised money via GoFundMe, which Ford used to pay for security for herself and her family. She planned to donate any funds she did not use to charities that support female victims of sexual assault.

TERMINOLOGY

In this book, I examine the use of digital technology to harm others. Do we call it cyberbullying, cyber-harassment, cyberaggression, or digital aggression? Why do the precise words matter? Although I write about cyberbullying (because it is the most widely used term), it is not the term I prefer (see Bauman, Underwood, & Card, 2013). First, it has the connotation of a childhood behavior, and what we are concerned with is hardly confined to childhood. Second, when we use that term, we should ensure the behaviors of interest meet the accepted standard for "bullying," which are (1) intentional aggression, (2) repeated over time, and (3) in which there is a power differential (physical, social, or other) between the perpetrator and target. In the digital context, these criteria are difficult to determine; there has also been considerable debate about how these criteria might manifest. For example, how does one determine the intent of an action? The perpetrator might conceivably regard an action as a joke, intended to amuse, while the observer may consider the action/comment to be crass or even intimidating. Further, a posting on social media could be forwarded, reposted or re-tweeted, by persons other than the original poster. In that situation, the action is repeated, but by other than the initial aggressor. Chatzalou et al. (2017) distinguish cyberbullying from cyberaggression by focusing on the "repeated" element, suggesting that cyberbullying is a more concerted campaign against the target and cyberaggression is a single incident.

Some scholars (e.g., Ybarra & Mitchell, 2007) prefer the term *cyber-harassment*, as it is less commonly associated with childhood, and does not have such restrictive defining characteristics. In general, cyber-harassment refers to actions (in the digital arena) that are ongoing and continuing despite being unwelcome. Legally, when this behavior is based on protected status (usually gender, race/ethnicity, sexual orientation, national origin, etc.), legal prohibitions apply, and the actions can be the basis of a lawsuit.

It seems that cyberaggression (Bauman et al., 2013) encompasses the kind of harmful behaviors of interest in this book. But Burt and Alhabash (2017) make a persuasive case for the difference between cyberbullying and digital aggression, arguing that "digital" is a broader term that would include such behaviors as aggression via text messaging. I quote their definition here, as I consider it to be my operational definition. "Digital aggression is generally defined as the use of information communication technologies . . . to intentionally inflict harm on others" (p. 125).

WEB 2.0

Although the internet has been widely used for decades now, the advent of Web 2.0 opened the doors to digital aggression in ways that were not possible prior to that innovation. The term *Web 2.0* was coined in 1999 by Darcy DiNucci and entered the popular lexicon in 2004, when it was used at a media conference by Tim O'Reilly and Dale Dougherty (Aced-Toledano, 2013). Web 2.0 refers to the way the internet is used interactively, including free e-mail accounts, online banking and bill paying, shopping, online dating sites, job seeking, photo storage, music access and storage, and other activities. Prior to this technological innovation, the World Wide Web was largely one-directional, with information available to be absorbed by passive consumers. To post content, one needed specific training in computer science, at a minimum the ability to write code (e.g., html).

> Although the internet has been widely used for decades now, the advent of Web 2.0 opened the doors to digital aggression in ways that were not possible prior to that innovation.

The most distinctive characteristic of Web 2.0 is the opportunity for users to contribute content, such as text, images, audio, video, and to edit and comment on other user-generated content (e.g., wikis). That is, the web became interactive; visitors were not merely passive consumers, but active participants. Education has embraced Web 2.0; students are able to pursue degrees without leaving their homes; they can submit papers, take quizzes, participate in discussions, view videos.

Today the comments of other shoppers help us decide whether to make an online purchase. Book reviews by other readers offer opinions and critiques that help us select the next book to read. Ordinary people (without computer science degrees) now create blogs (online journals) and otherwise publish content for a wide audience. In addition, the content on news sites, video-sharing sites, and elsewhere online allows for user-generated comments on content. Perhaps most important, this technological advance was necessary for the introduction and proliferation of social networking sites, which are interactive by definition. The subsequent increase in internet accessibility via mobile phones allowed for almost constant connectivity and use of these technologies, including for the purposes of digital aggression. Interactivity attracts attention to content because the viewer can actively engage with the content and ideas.

This is not to suggest that Web 2.0 technology is the cause of digital aggression, or that it was not possible prior to its proliferation. I maintain that once cyberspace became broadly participatory and interactive, the array of platforms available gave a public voice to anyone with access to the internet—and some of those chose to become aggressive in that context.

PLATFORMS FOR CYBERAGGRESSION

There are few online tools developed for the sole purpose of aggression. However, almost any type of interactive platform can be appropriated for that purpose. Here I provide an overview of the kinds of sites and apps that are widely used.

First, there are the news sites. Many online news sites are companions to longtime print newspapers (such as the *New York Times, Washington Post, Wall Street Journal, Christian Science Monitor, USA Today*), while others are affiliated with TV news (e.g., PBS, CNN, BBC), or are online-only news portals (e.g., brietbart.com, huffingtonpost.com, mashable.com, slate.com, politico.com, buzzfeed.com, and 29 others in 2017) (Pew Research Center, 2018). Recall that print newspapers publish letters to the editor from readers who comment on content, and OpEds, which are usually granted a bit more space, are also available. Thus, online news sites are not unique in offering a venue to consumers of content to post their responses to what they read. What is unique is the number of comments and the inability to realistically monitor those for "appropriateness." In fact, some sites terminated their comment sections because of the toxicity of the postings (Green, 2018). NPR ended the comments feature after eight years, finding that trolls (troublemakers whose goal is to be offensive and disruptive) dominated many comment threads and offended other users. NPR discovered that less than 1% of visitors submitted comments. Within that group, more than half of comments came from a small group of contributors, whose views dominated the site. *Popular Science* also removed its comments section, citing research that concluded that readers exposed to negative and unkind comments were less trusting of the content of the news reported on the site (Daum, 2013). The researchers dubbed their discovery "the nasty effects."

Social networking sites are designed to facilitate communication with other people, and/or to locate other people who share interests or history. In many cases, the people who interact via these social networking sites know each other in the offline world, but many also use the sites to expand their social networks. Facebook (2.38 billion active users as of March 2019, and 1.3 billion using Facebook's mobile messenger app in 2019) is an example of this type of site, as are LinkedIn (303 million active users) and Google + (395 million active accounts), WhatsApp (1.6 billion active users), and Reddit (330 million active users) (Stout, 2019). Each of these sites has unique affordances, but many users have accounts on multiple sites.

Microblogging sites allow users to post brief content and to create and use hashtags (a way to facilitate searching for posts with a specific topic without having a predetermined label) to link posts. These sites, like the social networking sites, allow users to "follow" or "subscribe" to posts by other users, to reply or comment publicly, or to send direct private messages to other users. Twitter (395 million active users) and Tumblr (23.2 million U.S. users) are the best known of these sites. For users of Twitter who want to organize tweets, management tools, such as Tweetdeck, are available.

For those who wish to publish blogs (Statista.com reported that in 2015 there were 28.3 million bloggers who posted monthly or more often), there are content management systems such as Wordpress, with 41.7 new posts each month (Barron, 2019). Blogspot.com, wix.com, and weebly.com are other popular platforms for this task. Bloggers not only post their own content but can link to other content or websites as well. Comments are often a feature of blogs.

Photo and media sharing is a very popular form of social media, and it is almost impossible to find a cell phone that does not include a camera for still and moving images. There is some debate about when the first phone with camera was available, but a Sanyo phone with camera became available in the United States in 2002. In the next few years, manufacturers, vying for a share of this booming market, increased the features and image quality available on these devices. Common platforms on which to share photos are Instagram (111.54 million monthly mobile users), Flickr, Snapchat (255 million active users), and Pinterest (200 million active users). Video-sharing platforms include YouTube (1.9 billion active users) and Vimeo (917,000 subscribers worldwide) among others. As with most social media platforms, commenting is a popular feature of the sites.

FREE SPEECH

As I hope is obvious, there are seemingly endless options for posting content, including aggressive or harmful content. Most social media sites have user agreements that specify what is acceptable on the site and have mechanisms for reporting content considered to be in violation of those terms. There are frequent requests of social media sites and blog hosts and others to remove content or to prohibit certain categories of content on the sites. This has been quite contentious, and whether the site does or does not take action, they will be subject to criticism. For example, Mark Zuckerberg, CEO of Facebook, chose to permit conspiracy theories and Holocaust denials to be posted on that site, and was subject to strident censure for that decision. What makes these decisions challenging is the basic freedom of speech guaranteed by our Constitution, and the subjective nature of deciding what is objectionable or worse.

A particularly unfortunate and tragic situation is that of Leonard Pozner, whose six-year-old son was killed in the Sandy Hook Elementary School shooting (Maheshwari & Herrman, 2018). Aside from the very painful loss of his young child, Pozner has had to ensure the online campaign from conspiracy theorists who claim the shootings did not really happen. He has pressured tech companies to restrict conspiracy theorists from their sites; has sued Alex Jones of Infowars, a primary promoter of the theory that Sandy Hook was a hoax; and has diligently reported every website and platform that posts these lies. Of course, each platform has different user agreements and policies and procedures, and the number of posts is overwhelming. Pozner's diligence has resulted in Facebook, Amazon, and Google removing some of this material, while Twitter has not. Other sites simply ignore him. He has struggled mightily against Word Press.com, which hosts blogs. The parent company that owns this site has said that untrue content and conspiracy theories are not prohibited from its site, so it has refused to take action to remove any of the offending posts. Pozner has been creative about his campaign and has been able to make copyright infringement claims when his son's images have been used. The only removal WordPress agreed to was to delete personal information such as addresses for Pozner. This story and the legal ramifications are more complex than what I have presented here, but I hope the point is clear: the digital landscape is in many ways a "wild west" where there are few rules to rein in the outlaws who can be unfathomably cruel.

The First Amendment to the U.S. Constitution prohibits any law "abridging the freedom of speech." This is the foundation for arguments that portray any attempts to restrict or limit content on the web to be a violation of the Constitution. However, this right is not absolute, and courts have upheld laws that delineate several types of "unprotected speech." Note that the Constitution restricts the government's behavior; individuals or businesses are not constrained in the same way. A detailed discussion of the history and legal precedents relevant to this issue is beyond the scope of this book. However, a brief summary will be important to understanding subsequent chapters.

Incitement to an illegal or harmful act is not protected by this amendment. States may legislate restrictions on "fighting words,"—speech that incites violence or urges listeners to commit crimes. The "average citizen" is the standard for evaluating the likelihood of speech to provoke a violent reaction. A famous example given in a Supreme Court challenge to freedom of speech was that of Justice Oliver Wendell Holmes, who noted that when the speech in question causes a "clear and present danger," as would be the case if someone shouted "fire" in a crowded theater when there was no fire, such a danger exists. The precedent has been interpreted somewhat differently in times of war, and a more stringent protection of speech has been noted in rulings in the past 50 years. The clear or present danger has been defined as potentially causing *imminent* harm and having the *intent* to cause immediate illegal action.

Another type of unprotected speech is *obscenity,* but the reader will recognize the difficulty in having a consensus definition of obscenity. The current criterion for deeming material to be obscene is the average person (a community standard based on a national standard) would agree that it is obscene, that the material presents sexual conduct in an offensive way per state law, and the material lacks other value (literary, artistic, etc.)

However, child pornography is not protected speech, nor is slander or libel, blackmail, perjury, invitations to commit crimes (recruitment of a "hit man"), nor are true threats protected speech. A true threat indicates a *serious* intention to commit violence against an identifiable target. That means that speech can be abusive or offensive but protected. This is likely the nature of the most frequent examples of cyberaggression. I will delve more deeply into this topic in Chapter 8.

RELEVANT RESEARCH

Research on cyberaggression has mainly focused on children and adolescents and has been largely descriptive in nature. Although some studies found gender differences in the prevalence of cyberbullying, others did not, and the jury is still out. In general, experts agree that cyberbullying peaks in middle school (as does traditional bullying), but one study reported that 30% of its sample had their first experience of cyberbullying in college (Kowalski, Giumetti, Schroeder, & Reese, 2012). The one consistent finding is that young people who are, or are thought to be, LGBT are at high risk for being victimized online. There is also agreement that there are negative consequences for cyberbullying involvement, including declines in school performance and increases in truancy, depressive symptoms, suicidal ideation, antisocial or delinquent behavior. There is considerable overlap between traditional bullying, with perpetrators often using both methods and targets being attacked in both contexts. There is some evidence that traditional victims turn to cyberspace to retaliate and thus become cyberbullies, but the evidence is not strong for this.

One context in which cyberaggression is common is in online gaming, especially massively multiplayer online games (MMOGs; Warner & Raiter, 2005). The gaming world attracts many adult players and should not be overlooked when studying cyberaggression.

A few studies have looked at cyberbullying in the workplace (e.g., Gardner et al., 2016; Piotrowski, 2012; Privitera & Campbell, 2009). There is agreement that cyberaggression in the workplace is almost always accompanied by more traditional bullying in the work setting, and that it occurs less frequently than face-to-face forms of bullying and harassment. Piotrowski (2012, p. 49) indicates that much of the digital abuse that occurs is in the form of "obsessive relational intrusion . . . that can be considered cyberstalking." He urges companies to develop clear policies regarding both workplace bullying and cyberbullying, and to develop policies for intervening with employees found to be in violation.

What the research has yet to address is how to reduce the harm from cyberaggression. Preventing cyberaggression is a worthy goal, but the reality is that behavior is unlikely to disappear. Thus, we need to focus on understanding the behavior and on developing strategies to manage reactions and responses to minimize the harmful effects, both tangible (e.g., losing a job) and psychological (e.g., being anxious and depressed).

SUMMARY

This chapter provided the backdrop for the rest of the book. I reminded readers of the omnipresent technology in our society, which leaves us all vulnerable to aggression in cyberspace. I provided evidence that cyberaggression is a serious problem, and that there are numerous ways in which the determined aggressor can express their views, ugly and nasty as they may be. The First Amendment ensures that people have the right to voice their thoughts and opinions, with very few restrictions. Research is sparse regarding this topic as it relates to adults; scholarly literature on cyberbullying among children and adolescents is more robust. Nevertheless, there is no research to support a specific strategy or program for damage control or building resistance. I hope the remainder of the book will lead us in that direction.

At the end of each chapter, I include stories of people who have been targets of digital aggression. The stories sometimes include real names, but often do not, at the request of the protagonist. The stories do not always illustrate the topic of the chapter, but each one reveals the damage done to targets, and some show how targets manage the challenges posed by digital aggression.

SAIDA GRUNDY'S STORY

Saida Grundy is an assistant professor at Boston University, a race scholar, a feminist, a sociologist, and one of the few Black faculty at her institution (5.7% in 2018). She is also a passionate, articulate, confident woman who is unafraid to speak her truth. Furthermore, she is a student of history, who recognizes in our history the origin of the issues we confront in the current moment. Her membership in this small group of Black, female academics is directly related to her experience of cyberaggression that is the subject of this story.

As an undergraduate, Saida Grundy attended Spelman College, a historically Black college for women, a prestigious institution ranked highly on a number of metrics. After graduation, she attended the University of Michigan for graduate studies leading to her PhD. A recent profile of racial diversity at the school indicates 4.3% of undergraduates at Michigan identify as Black or African American. This means that in graduate school, unlike at Spelman, Grundy was one of a small minority group and felt disconnected from people and issues that were important to her. One of the ways she attempted to relieve her isolation was to use Twitter to connect with others like her, and she found it gratifying not to feel left out of an important circle of like-minded others. Upon completion of her PhD, Grundy accepted a position as an assistant professor at Boston University. Her official start date was July 1, 2015.

Although she had not been targeted personally prior to this incident of digital attacks, she does recall that because her parents were very active in promoting Martin Luther King Day as a holiday, they received racist threats that terrified young Saida. However, being raised by parents who fought for what they believed despite the backlash from others, she learned that taking a stand, even at a personal price, is what defines a moral human being. Like many of us, Grundy was not diligent about privacy settings on all of her social media accounts. And, since she was on the job market, she had profiles and contact information available so that potential employers could locate her information. That made her particularly vulnerable to doxing and threats that included threats to her parents at their home.

In May 2015, she made some statements on Twitter without realizing the size or nature of the audience that would see them. Some considered those statements to be provocative or controversial, and others labeled them racist. Grundy believes it was not chance or random bad luck that she was targeted for the online and media campaign to discredit her. Campus Reform is a right-wing group dedicated to "exposing liberal bias" on college campuses, and Peter Hasson was a "campus correspondent" at the time of the Grundy campaign. His articles on the site attacked people whom he saw as "liberal"—a pejorative term for him. He clearly expended considerable time and energy looking on Twitter and other social media for people to "expose." Then, the African American Studies department updated its faculty page to include the incoming Grundy. The Campus Reform correspondent likely regularly checked such pages to detect potential targets, and then he began his surveillance. The two of Grundy's posts that he seized upon were: "White masculinity isn't a problem for America's colleges, white masculinity is THE problem for America's colleges," Grundy tweeted in March. And "Every MLK week I commit myself to not spending a dime in white-owned businesses. And every year I find it nearly impossible."

It is ironic that I, a White woman, am writing this as the furor over the reports of sexual assault by the privileged White male nominee for a lifetime chair on the Supreme Court is flooding the news. What I hear (to no surprise) is more privileged White men discounting or besmirching the reputations of the women who have courageously spoken up about their traumatic experiences, and then repeating the worn-out victim-blaming narratives that have been stock in trade for White males. And these men get to evaluate the truth of women's stories. And, in a similar vein, White people were the ones to decide that Grundy's comments are both inappropriate and racist.

It is important to consider the political and racial context at the time this situation was unfolding. Donald Trump was on the scene garnering significant publicity with his Make America Great Again campaign. His racism was well documented, and his rise on the public stage legitimized the views of those who shared his ideas. His unwillingness to discredit White supremacists emboldened those who had held such views privately to speak publicly. See Chapter 3 for more on this topic.

Hasson went to great lengths to demean Grundy and to stir up his base to add to the negative and vindictive comments. He found and read her dissertation, which he said also included derogatory comments about White men. Note that dissertations must be approved by a committee of scholars, who take their role—to certify that a dissertation reflects quality scholarship—very seriously. Clearly the members of her committee, all doctoral-level scholars, did not take exception to the dissertation, but Campus Reform undergraduate students considered themselves to be a worthy judge of her work. It is very likely the case that this Campus Reformer rallied supporters to contact the president of Boston University, demanding that Grundy be terminated. He also tweeted the posts (with commentary) to news outlets, so that her tweets were covered on Fox News and other outlets. It is notable that in one of his tweets, he referred to Grundy as a "girl."

The university president, Robert Brown, wrote an open letter in which he confirmed Grundy's right to express her views. He said, "Boston University does not condone racism or bigotry in any form, and we are committed to maintaining an educational environment that is free from bias, fully inclusive, and open to wide-ranging discussions," and "at Boston University, we acknowledge Grundy's right to hold and express her opinions." "I understand there is a broader context to Grundy's tweets and that, as a scholar, she has the right to pursue her research, formulate her views, and challenge the rest of us to think differently about race relations," he said. Grundy made a public apology, saying "I regret that my personal passion about issues surrounding these events led me to speak about them indelicately," but that did not stop her tormentors. On Instagram, some of her "critics" referred to her as n****r, and proclaimed she was the real racist.

Furthermore, Grundy's start date at the university was publicized on social media. Coincidentally, on that night, the building in which her department is located was broken into and posters designed to denigrate her were put on the walls. The culprits actually filmed themselves doing this, appearing quite gleeful and proud of themselves, and posted the video on social media. Police never arrested or charged the culprits.

Grundy continued to be taunted on Twitter and received messages such as "We have a surprise for you Grundy," and attempts to hack into her e-mail account were detected. She experienced considerable anxiety and changed her passwords and addresses; the campus police eventually installed a panic button in her office, shadowed her, and monitored her e-mails. One of the taunts, sent by a White man from Delaware said, "You do something about Grundy or I will."

I asked Grundy how she weathered such a firestorm. One strategy was not to read all the posts (see Liam Hackett's profile for similar approach). Despite limiting her intake of the harsh rhetoric, she felt as though she was being portrayed as a "big bad black witch" and as a girl who does not deserve respect. She experienced a degree of public exposure and criticism that would wither less-determined persons. Her strong convictions kept her from capitulating and brought forward many Black academics who reached out to her and remain part of her circle today. She has also discovered she has some strong allies on her campus. These more seasoned scholars helped Grundy frame these events as the inevitable initiation to the reality of being a highly educated Black person. One of the lingering effects of these events is the disappointment at not being able to have clean interactions when she meets new people, as they are likely to have heard of her and formed impressions in advance of any contact with her. She says the aggressors "took away [my] personhood."

And it's not over. Every few months, when the news is slow, people seeking a diversion dredge up the original conflagration and regurgitate it. Grundy then will experience a surge of digital aggression, including comments such as "better watch your ass."

This story is not the anomaly it should be. In September 2018, for example, Kiah Morris, a Black female legislator in Vermont resigned her position due to the barrage of racial harassment she received, much of it on social media with racist epithets and offensive images. Social media enhances the ability of those who seek to demean powerful persons of color and women and such people have a tool in their pockets with which to do so.

Saida Grundy's experience was not caused by social media, but it was certainly enabled by it, and both the positive and harmful elements were at play. The doctoral candidate Grundy sought a way to foster important relationships when she was isolated from peers, and that was helpful—that is, until she posted some comments that were seized upon to promulgate a highly charged racist platform. The speed with which Twitter disseminates posts and the size of the audience that is reached ensured that she was attacked harshly and repeatedly. The ability of savvy internet users to find personal information with which to harass a target adds to the potential damage and allows the digital aggression to easily spill over into offline arenas.

2

Theories of Aggression

What is the nature of the behavior we are trying to understand? It seems prudent to examine the concept of "aggression" before we discuss how that behavior manifests in the current digital universe. Generally, aggression is defined as behavior that is intended to harm another who does not wish to be harmed. Although widely accepted, the challenge with this definition is that *intent* is not observable but must be inferred from the outcome. This is particularly difficult to determine when the identity of the aggressive party is unknown, as might be the case in cyberspace. It is not unusual for the sender (or poster) of a message to believe it was playful or humorous when the recipient is hurt and offended. Is that aggression?

Two types of aggression are distinguished: *instrumental* or proactive aggression, and *reactive* aggression. The former refers to aggression that is deliberate and directed toward a goal, such as getting money (in a robbery) or increasing one's social standing or status, as in cyber-aggression, while the latter describes an impulsive, usually emotional response to an actual or perceived attack. We often see both in social media, and in fact the president's tweets provide examples of both. Donald Trump has attacked those with whom he is unhappy (e.g., Attorney General Jeff Sessions, Ilhan Omar) by tweeting criticisms, belittling them, and modeling instrumental aggression. He often makes disparaging comments about journalists and the media, who he believes are unfair to him. When Trump perceives he has been unfairly treated, he frequently strikes out by targeting the source with demeaning names and accusations of foul play (reactive aggression).

There are numerous theories that purport to explain human aggression, and it is beyond the scope of this book to review all of those. I acknowledge a degree of selection bias, in that I cover the theories I find most useful—and least complicated—for understanding cyberaggression. For each, I consider how it applies to and sheds light on the type of aggressive behavior we are concerned with in this book. Although these theories (with two exceptions) were developed prior to the advent of digital technology, it is a testimony to their utility that they contribute to our efforts to understand this relatively recent incarnation of human aggression.

INSTINCT OR DRIVE THEORIES

Sigmund Freud

Sigmund Freud originally suggested that aggression was the result of the blocking of the life force or instinct toward pleasure-seeking and avoidance of pain.[1] However, after living through the incredible destruction of life in World War I, Freud reconsidered his theory and came to believe that aggression is one of two competing universal innate human drives: *Eros*, the life force, and *Thanatos*, the striving for death. He theorized that organisms, including humans, seek peace—or a complete absence of tension (excitation)—which can be achieved only by self-destruction. Dennen (2005) explained that Freud's notion was that all organic life has a drive or instinct to return to an earlier state of being (nonexistence). However, the energy of Eros (libido) counteracts that drive by redirecting the force outward as aggression toward others (Bandura, 1973; Baron & Richardson, 1994; Berkowitz, 1993). That means that our aggression toward others keeps us from aggressing toward ourselves.

A related concept of Freud's bears noting. *Catharsis* refers to the expression of intense emotions, the release of emotional energy, which serves to bring calm and a reduction in tension. From this perspective, watching violent events (football, boxing, action movies, etc.) is a cathartic experience that reduces the need for aggressive behavior. I wonder if observing online incivility or cyberaggression provides a cathartic release, or whether it is more likely to act as a model of acceptable behavior. Social learning theory (discussed later in the chapter) addresses that question.

Konrad Lorenz

Konrad Lorenz, a famous ethologist, considered human aggression to be an *instinctual* act (1966). Lorenz's view derives from Darwinian principles and his own study of the animal kingdom. He focused on the survival value of the behavior. He proposed that for our ancestors, aggression functioned to disperse the population so that resources would be available to all, and to ensure that the most successful genetic attributes were those that were passed on to subsequent generations. Aggression would have increased the chances of survival by ensuring that individuals had access to food, desirable mates, and territory. Thus, the aggressive members of our species were more likely to reproduce and pass their genes on to their progeny. The preservation of the species is also assisted by a hierarchical social structure that may require aggression to ensure the preservation of that hierarchy. Consider that one of the motives for cyberaggression is to elevate or preserve the social status of the aggressor; this theory may help explain the origin of that need.

One final point about Lorenz's contribution: He posited that the functions of aggression (preservation of species) developed in our primitive ancestors. Interestingly, he observed that in mammals that fight over territory or access to a fertile female, the outcome is rarely death for the weaker combatant. The weaker member will display a behavior signaling his capitulation (usually exposing a vulnerable body part—neck or belly) and the stronger one backs off, having achieved the goal of dominance. Lorenz believed that early man was unlikely to have such methods of inhibiting aggression because they usually did not have the physical capacity to destroy the opponent—that is, until the use of weapons appeared on the scene. Thus, what originated as a survival mechanism now persists despite the evolution of the species.[2]

Although both Freud and Lorenz were strongly influenced by Darwin's theory, Lorenz did not agree with the notion of a death instinct. The important feature of these theories is that both saw aggression as internally caused by in-born characteristics of our species. Lorenz went on to say that the energy propelling this instinct could build up if not released appropriately (as in catharsis?) and could then find outlets that are inappropriate. This notion has been described as a hydraulic model, mimicking the behavior of water under pressure and is similar to Freud's notion of displacement, which describes the unconscious process by which we direct an impulse away from a dangerous object toward a safer one. This is the classic "kick-the-dog" scenario, in which a worker is furious at the boss, but knows that expressing that anger in the workplace could lead to unemployment. The anger is released at the first available "safe" target, the loyal dog.

One of the criticisms of these theories is that there is no supporting empirical evidence of these instincts. Others have been skeptical of Lorenz's inferences about human aggression because they are based on his studies of other animals, not humans. Critics of Freud dispute the death instinct (which cannot be observed), but agree that there is an instinct toward aggression, which is observed.

It is easy to dismiss these theories as irrelevant to cyberbullying and aggression, but perhaps there are features of these views that could promote our understanding. Whether aggression is an instinct or a drive seems less important than the notion that it is definitely present in the human genetic template. Like other heritable characteristics, it is likely to vary among individuals, so that within members of the species we have varying degrees of aggressive impulses and behaviors. In most cases, people express their aggressive impulses through socially sanctioned avenues, but when those avenues are unavailable, they might actively seek alternative outlets. Enter cyberspace, with opportunities galore to be aggressive, and an ethos that appears to be increasingly accepting of such behavior.

> Enter cyberspace, with opportunities galore to be aggressive, and an ethos that appears to be increasingly accepting of such behavior.

FRUSTRATION-AGGRESSION HYPOTHESIS

A different view of aggression that does not rely on evolution or biology is that of Dollard and Miller (1939). Their frustration-aggression hypothesis posits that humans aggress when they are frustrated—that is, when they are prevented from attaining a goal that they expected to achieve. The strength of the impulse to act aggressively is related to the degree of satisfaction expected from the achievement of the goal, the completeness with which the goal is blocked, and the frequency with which this has happened. The absolute connection (frustration leads to aggression always, and aggression is always caused by frustration) in the original theory led to some of the proponents to moderate the theory, as it is apparent that there are many ways in addition to aggression that people react to frustration—one of which is cyberaggression.

Gurr (2011) reexamined his theory of political rebellion first published in 1970 (Gurr, 1970). His theory builds on the frustration-aggression hypothesis, and although it focuses on violent actions by a "collective," it provides a lens that might be informative for our purposes. The basic premise is that collective violence is fueled by a specific type of frustration—deprivation and discontent. In Gurr's lexicon, relative deprivation is the perception that there is a gap between what one believes is their due and what they can achieve in the current societal context. Such discontent can be politicized (directed toward those in power), and the impetus to violence has fertile ground in which to grow.

How that type of frustration manifests, according to Gurr (2011), is a function of the tension produced by the unpleasant feelings. Humans, having the ability to act aggressively, will do so because it is "an inherently satisfying response to the tension built up through frustration" (p. 23). Although collective physical violence is one possible outcome, I contend that on an individual level, those members of society who experience relative deprivation (those who feel threatened by increased participation of minorities in society and in politics, whose jobs are becoming obsolete, who believe that they are entitled to more resources and power than are forthcoming) may find that digital technology provides a readily available platform for "striking out" (p. 23).

SOCIAL LEARNING THEORY

This theory, proposed by Albert Bandura (1971, 1973), argues that humans have the capacity to behave aggressively, but unlike drive theories discussed earlier, Bandura proposed that this behavior is learned. People learn from experience—either their own or others'—by observing the consequences of a given behavior. If those are positive, the behavior is likely to be repeated and if those are unpleasant or negative, repetition is less likely. Because they also have the capacity for thought, humans can anticipate the likely consequences of an action and decide how to act based on those predicted results. Bandura also proclaimed that human beings have considerable control over their own behavior. They are not controlled by drives or instincts, nor is an external event (frustration) an inevitable precursor of aggression. He disputed the Freudian principle that catharsis after observing aggressive behavior reduces aggression. On the contrary, he believed that viewing aggressive behavior is more likely to lead to modeling (learning) that behavior than reducing it.

From learning theory, Bandura agrees that when the consequence of a behavior is positive or pleasurable, there is increased likelihood the behavior will be repeated. Conversely, if the consequence is unpleasant or painful, repetition is less likely (operant conditioning). Since humans can anticipate, they are able to think about possible consequences without experiencing them directly. Another key element of the learning process is the importance of modeling. Humans can and do learn many behaviors by observing and imitating models. We learn to speak that way, and we also learn what social behaviors are expected by following the example of appropriate models. In other words, when a child observes aggressive behavior in others, the child notes whether the aggression leads to positive or negative consequences and behaves in ways that will maximize the positive consequences. Children learn from their own aggressive behavior and its consequences, too, and draw conclusions about its usefulness in achieving their goals and positive outcomes.

Bandura described the process by which models influence behavior. Features of the model that enhance that influence include the power and attractiveness of the model. In the case of Trump, observers cannot deny the enormous power he wields as the president of the world's most powerful country. The person observing the model gathers information about the observed behavior. They note whether the behavior is positively reinforced in the model. Bandura's famous experiments with the Bobo doll, in which children viewed various models' behavior with the doll and then had the opportunity to play with it, showed how important modeling is in learning aggressive behavior. Those who observed the aggressive models behaved significantly more aggressively when given the opportunity to play with Bobo.

If someone tweets offensive or defamatory comments, what is the consequence? In the case of Trump, that seems to be increased attention. During his campaign, his tweets attracted a loyal group of supporters who have been steadfast even in the face of strong criticism of his behavior. The observer also sees how other people react to the model's behavior. If others are offended and retreat from the aggressive person, that is useful information. If, however, others adopt the behavior (as do other political figures, for example) the learner is more inclined to imitate the behavior.

An important and relevant concept from social learning theory is that of *moral disengagement*. Because it is so germane to the discussion of the cyberbully in chief, I discuss that in some detail in the next chapter.

SOCIAL MEDIA CYBERBULLYING MODEL

An offshoot, or modification of social learning theory, the social media cyberbullying model (SMCBM; Lowry, Zhang, Wang, & Siponen, 2016) takes the unique context of the digital world and social media into account. Their theory also derives from theories of criminal behavior, notably that of Akers (2011). The authors believed that prior attempts to use existing theories to understand cyberbullying suffered from not taking the social media environment into account.

Criminals typically associate with other criminals and learn and reinforce criminal social norms from each other. I suspect this *differential association* effect may contribute to the high rates of recidivism among released prisoners. The basic idea is that one learns to behave from others in their social milieu; if one associates online with cyberbullies, they are more likely to adopt that behavior than if they associate with those who exhibit exemplary netiquette. A social media user also attends to the consequences of cyberbullying they experience or observe. This is called *differential reinforcement*. From learning theory, we know that we are likely to adopt behaviors that are reinforced and to avoid behaviors that are punished. These cognitive processes lead one to define a given behavior in a way that renders it acceptable (even if only in specific situations) or not. Then we must include the *social structure* of a given environment. Among the various social media platforms, there are some that are known as places where cyberbullying and trolling are commonplace (e.g., 4chan, Reddit, Tumblr), even expected, whereas other sites, while not free of cyberbullying are less attractive to those with harm in mind (e.g., Facebook). Depending on which sites one visits most frequently, the social structure will vary. Lowry et al. (2016) note that the social environment online is quite different from offline; online social groups can be huge, geographically and demographically diverse, with varying attitudes toward cyberbullying behaviors. Some sites have moderators who attempt to control toxic content, while others wait to receive user complaints. The type and frequency of cyberbullying also varies among social media communities.

Lowry et al. (2016) built the SMCBM around what they see as the critical component of social media–perceived anonymity. These scholars believe that this unique aspect of social media leads to a sense of confidence that an individual cyberbully cannot be identified, and that because there are so many people in the community, an individual's feelings of responsibility are diffused. Furthermore, because a subscriber usually does not know others in the community very well, they assume no one knows them well enough to identify them either, and count on the mysteries of technology infrastructure to keep them anonymous. Five factors are proposed to explain why these features enable cyberbullying: (1) many social media sites allow users to post under pseudonyms, or to create phony identities, allowing them to be anonymous; (2) sophisticated users can employ other technological techniques to hide identities; (3) people are more likely to attack someone they don't know; (4) the vast size of social media audiences allows cyberbullies to attack people to whom they do not have offline access; and (5) cyberbullies are unlikely to be prosecuted or even sanctioned in most cases.

While I think this theory is commendable for its incorporation of affordances of social media to understand adult cyberbullying behavior,

I find several assumptions to be problematic. First, although anonymity is often touted as an enticement for cyberbullies, cyberbullies are not always anonymous (e.g., Bauman, 2010; Holfeld & Grabe, 2012; Li, 2007; Ybarra & Mitchell, 2004b).[3] This theory completely ignores that fact and does not account for cyberbullying by known perpetrators. For example, most people would agree that Trump cyberbullies others who he perceives have slighted him in some way. Second, it is unclear how the authors determined that individuals are more likely to attack targets they do not know. The point of much cyberbullying is to harm or cause distress to someone because of some perceived factor. Trump has cyberbullied his opponents (e.g., Hillary Clinton and Barack Obama) and others whose statements or behavior displeases him (e.g., Jeff Sessions, James Comey, Justin Trudeau).

SOCIAL INFORMATION PROCESSING

Dodge (1986) and later Crick and Dodge (1994) proposed a model of how individuals interpret social situations, which determines how they act. Although the model appears to be linear, the 1994 revision recognized that steps can occur simultaneously or circularly (in which later steps influence earlier steps). The model also presupposes that we all have past experiences in our long-term memory and these memories are incorporated into general cognitive schemas (models or scripts) that underlie the way we process new situations. The model includes six steps. First, the information has to be encoded correctly. That means the information from the environment is noticed and attended to. The second step is the point at which that information is interpreted. It is at this step that the *hostile attribution bias* may be invoked. A goal is selected in the third step, while in the fourth step, one considers the possible behaviors. In step five, those possible behaviors are evaluated, and in the final step, the chosen behavior is enacted.

The hostile attribution bias is an important feature in many digitally aggressive circumstances. This means that when a situation is somewhat ambiguous, the individual with a hostile attribution bias is likely to interpret the incident or message as aggressive, hostile, threatening, and so on. Social information processing (SIP) has not put forth an opposite attribution bias—I call it a Pollyanna bias. I have observed a number of individuals who in the same ambiguous circumstance will interpret the message or action as well-meaning, or even positive. These general tendencies to view the world as a hostile or benevolent place certainly influence one's online behavior.

In a case of potential digital aggression, the steps might look like this: (1) I notice an ambiguous post on my Facebook wall and focus my attention on it. Note there are many posts I do not attend to, so something about that post (perhaps the name of the poster, the hashtag, my physiological reaction) interacts with my internal state to draw my attention there. (2) Based on my previous experience and cognitive schema, I have developed a hostile attribution bias, so I interpret this post as insulting and demeaning. In making this interpretation, I consider my past experience with the poster and how I believe others would evaluate the post. (3) I determine that my goal is to preserve my reputation and status as a respected professor. (4), I consider whether to ignore the post and move on, respond to the post in a direct way (e.g., "I consider that post to be an insult and demand an apology"), unfriend the poster, hide the poster, or post a nasty reply ("This post reveals your inferior intelligence and faulty judgment"). (5) I select what I evaluate as the best option. And (6) Finally, I enact that behavior. Note that this process is largely out of awareness and occurs in seconds—not a lengthy deliberative reflection.

I contend that Trump behaves in a way that displays a hostile attribution bias that fuels his behavior on and offline. For example, when a media journalist persisted in asking for information during a press conference, Trump had him removed and revoked his White House press credentials (which were restored by a judge). In step 2, Trump likely perceived the question as intending to humiliate him or embarrass him and reacted to that hostile interpretation in an aggressive manner. Although this happened in a face-to-face encounter, the incident had wide play on social media, thanks largely to Trump's penchant for using that avenue for speaking out.

QUADRIPARTITE VIOLENCE TYPOLOGY

The cyber SIP theory adaptation proposed by Runions (2013) and tested by Runions, Salmivalli, Shaw, Burns, and Cross (2018) describes the ways in which an individual aggressor's motives and their degree of self-control interact with the features of cyberspace to explain cyberaggression. First, the theory considers the *motives* (reactive versus proactive [called appetitive in this approach]) and the degree of *self-control* (impulsive versus planned) involved. These two dimensions form four quadrants (Rage, Revenge, Reward, and Recreation) surrounded by two layers of Information and Communication Technology (ICT) characteristics that provide the context for cyberbullying. The inner layer includes features of the digital environment, and the outer layer shows the influences of the features of the potential cyberaggressor.

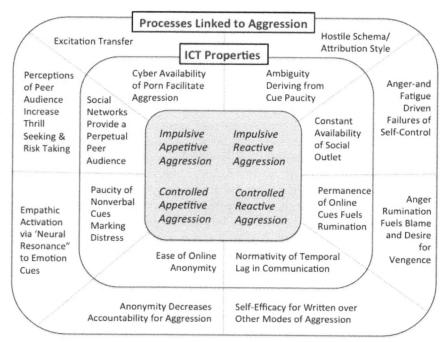

Figure 2.1 A motive and self-control model of cyberaggression linking ICT properties to processes relevant to a quadripartite violence typology-informed conceptualization of aggression. (From Runions, Kevin C. "Toward a conceptual model of motive and self-control in cyber-aggression: Rage, revenge, reward, and recreation." *Journal of Youth and Adolescence*, 42(5), 2013, 753. Copyright (c) 2013, Springer Science Business Media New York. Used by permission.)

SOCIAL ECOLOGICAL THEORY

Early work on bullying and aggression focused on the individuals involved and sought to identify characteristics of bullies and victims that predisposed them to such behavior. Urie Bronfenbrenner (1979, 1995), an American psychologist interested in child development, proposed an influential model that is widely applied in bullying research (e.g., Swearer & Espelage, 2004, 2011) and may be even more relevant to cyberbullying and cyberaggression.

Bronfenbrenner (2005) situated the individual at the center of a series of concentric circles. The circles represent layers of reciprocal influence on the developing person. The point is that we cannot understand the individual in isolation from the environment.

Surrounding the individual is the *microsystem* that contains the biological features, immediate context, including family, school, workplace, friends, neighborhoods, religious communities. The *mesosystem* involves the inter-actions among those systems. The *exosystem* encompasses the larger soci-etal institutions, such as the economy, political system, education, government. The *macrosystem* is the layer in which the cultural values and beliefs reside, all of which is encircled by the *chronosystem,* or the time in history in which the individual exists.

What this theory adds to our understanding is the impact of the histori-cal timeframe (the Trump campaign and presidency), and the political, government, and economic systems on individual behavior. The intensive use of social media is unique to Trump's presidency, and the governmental actions in his administration that hint at racism, classism, and disdain for facts and education influence individuals, especially those who feel disaf-fected by these systems. Often, they interact with others (family, friends) who share that dissatisfaction with the status quo, and the combined effect of these layers of influence may encourage or at least condone aggressive behavior using digital tools.

Johnson and Puplampu (2008) attempted to integrate technology into the social ecological framework. They proposed a techno-subsystem and situated it within the microsystem, or immediate environment. While that makes sense, it seems to me that in the decade since their proposal was published, the presence of technology permeates all the systems and should be seen as an overlay covering all the systems in the model.

SUMMARY

In this chapter, I provided an overview of the most prominent theories of aggression so that the reader has a context for the remaining chapters in the book. Although each theory makes some contribution to our under-standing of aggression in cyberspace, as yet there does not appear to be one dominant theory that fully explains the phenomenon.

LIAM HACKETT'S STORY

Lest we think that cyberaggression is a uniquely American phenome-non, we now look at an example from the United Kingdom, which is also a democracy experiencing political turmoil. Liam Hackett is a tall, attrac-tive, confident, self-assured, and congenial gay man in his late 20s. He is the youngest person to have ever received an honorary doctorate from Sussex University, in the United Kingdom, his alma mater. He is also the creator and CEO of a prominent global anti-bullying charity and someone whose impressive accomplishments belie his age. Given his mission to spare young people from the negative effects of bullying, it is perhaps ironic that he has been victimized by bullies throughout his life. A recent incident of cyberbullying is the subject of this profile, but a bit of history provides some background for that event.

Liam was raised in northern England by a single mother; his father has not been in his life since he left when Liam was three. When Liam was ten years old, a younger brother with high-functioning autism joined the family. Unfortunately, the marriage of Liam's mother and his brother's father ended in divorce, adding yet more disruption to Liam's childhood.

Liam's victimization by bullies began when he was in primary school. He was considered "different," was called a "girl," and was generally excluded by his peers. After one particularly brutal physical attack by three boys, the head teacher chose not to take action against the bullies because the mother of the lead bully was a prominent supporter of the school. The solution was for Liam to change schools, and the rest of primary school was less tumultuous.

In high school, the bullying resumed and escalated. He was subjected to homophobic epithets, was teased about his acne, and his shy and quiet demeanor made him a likely target. At one point, he was physically bullied severely when two boys held him down so the third attacker could bang Liam's head into the hood of a car. This attack resulted in hospitalization. Liam was also publicly humiliated when he messaged a boy he liked who he thought was gay and expressed his affection. The recipient of the message engaged in the conversation, and then took screenshots and displayed screenshots of the chats around the school, humiliating Liam. A female classmate he thought was a friend tried to remove his gym shorts in front of others, and the accumulation of these incidents left him feeling so hopeless and isolated that suicide was something he considered.

Rather than ending his life, Liam decided that he wanted to help others who experienced such degradation by bullies. At age 15, he came out to his mother, who was accepting and supportive. He used his MySpace page to escape his tormenters and encourage and help others who, like him, might be driven to contemplate suicide, or who felt pressure to "change." He wanted to make a statement that labels don't define a person, and that living authentically was necessary for one's mental health. He acquired a large audience online and decided to create his own website. He was heartened by comments and thanks expressed by his followers, and while he continued to use MySpace as a platform, he worked on his website, eventually receiving a small grant to develop it further.

In 2012, after graduating from university, he used what he learned studying business in high school, college, and university to turn his project into a charitable organization in order to have a broader influence on a societal level. At the same time, he created a digital marketing agency to support himself until the anti-bullying charity was well established.

Ditch the Label is now a very visible and respected charity globally, and Liam is the face of the organization. He does numerous media events and television appearances and has been very successful at getting his anti-bullying message out to a large swath of the public. At present, he is in the process of establishing an office in the United States, as many site visitors are from America, and he believes he can best serve that audience if there is a U.S. locus of operation.

The incident of cyberbullying began when Liam responded to a tweet by a lecturer at Sussex University, who suggested that there be a debate about whether transgender women should be allowed basic rights. Liam requested that the post be removed because guaranteeing basic rights to all is not up for debate. He was then inundated with abusive messages (more than 4,000 in a six-week period) calling him a rapist and pedophile, posting photos of him and urging him to kill himself, calling his office, claiming that ditchthelabel.org promoted suicide and groomed young people for sexual abuse. They posted fake reviews of his organization, found and published his personal information (address, phone number), and delivered a sustained assault on his reputation. Twitter was the primary platform on which this campaign was waged, although a forum thread was also used. He also received death threats, and there were posts offering to assist the perpetrator. Although there were also thanks from trans individuals who appreciated Liam's advocacy on their behalf, the torrent of attacks was overwhelming. Liam also realized that there are many quiet supporters who share his convictions and admire his efforts, but who don't vocalize their defense.

Because he knows that cyberbullies aim to get a reaction from their targets, Liam did not respond in order not to empower his abusers. He used the available reporting mechanisms in an attempt to get derogatory and defamatory posts removed, but the process is daunting at best. However, he became physically ill, had to involve the police (especially for protection when joining in the Pride Parade), and had to be careful to lock all doors and be aware of his surroundings. He eventually had to change his phone number, which, given the numerous ways our lives are linked to that number, created and continues to create enormous inconvenience. Because of his charitable organization and his business savvy, Liam had access to legal advice and had offers to defend him because of this notoriety. He realizes that most people do not have those advantages, and this awareness has fueled his passion to be the voice of those who have been bullied.

In a final effort to stop the cyberbullying that was impacting his offline and online life, Liam called the deputy vice chancellor at Sussex University and made a complaint about the lecturer. This official arranged a meeting, and Liam provided 150 pages of the horrific tweets and posts authored by this person. When confronted with the totality of her statements, she was horrified, realized she should know better, and the bullying stopped.

Despite this resolution, the incident generated some strategies going forward to minimize the damage from cyberbullying. Prior to this incident, Liam had blocked 7 people on Twitter. He has now blocked 1,954 accounts. He continues to use Twitter because it is the most topical social media site (he uses Facebook and Instagram for communicating with friends and family), and Twitter is important to getting out the Ditch the Label message and engaging stakeholders. So, he now has someone else go through his tweets and report offenses on his behalf. This minimizes the emotional pain that one experiences when exposed to online cruelty. Although one can attempt to develop a thick skin, no one is completely impervious to the kind of venomous content that can appear, and sparing oneself from viewing a torrent of torment is a wise protective move. Liam is passionate about his cause and continues to object to unfairness wherever it appears, including online. He recognizes that he is likely to receive waves of abuse after a tweet or comment that provokes those who favor hate speech and aggression. His new strategy will reduce the life disruption from these predictable reactions.

NOTES

1. This idea was later expanded upon by the proponents of the frustration-aggression hypothesis, discussed later in this chapter.

2. I think of this as analogous to an appendix in human anatomy. Obviously, the appendix served a purpose at one time, but I have lived most of my life without one, with no adverse effects.

3. These studies were based on samples of adolescents.

3

Cyberbully in Chief

Calvin Coolidge was the first president whose inauguration was heard over the radio (1929), Harry Truman was the first whose inaugural address was televised (1949), and John F. Kennedy's (1961) was the first to be viewed on color television. Prior to the invention and widespread use of radio, politicians had to travel the country to personally speak to as many voters as possible. Heads of state communicated in writing by mail or via messenger. At times, government officials from different countries met in person to discuss sensitive issues of mutual interest. Although these practices have not been completely abandoned, they are arguably less influential than in bygone years, since the public knows they can read about events online, watch them on television, and turn to social media for information and opinion.

Social media platforms allow politicians and others to communicate directly with their audience, without an intermediary (e.g., a journalist or television news reporter). A candidate, for example, can make statements designed to malign an opponent with the assurance that the unfiltered message will reach supporters. It is possible that some viewers will not take kindly to this tactic, but many seem to relish such attacks. According to Van Blokland (2017), angry or aggressive messages are favorably received by those who share the point of view of the tweeter but are unlikely to change the beliefs of someone with opposing views. The Anger Activation Model proposes that angry messages are persuasive for those in the audience who already share the position being promoted.

The campaign and tenure of Donald Trump has changed the way a head of state communicates with his or her constituency and the larger global audience. Trump has chosen Twitter to be his primary platform for disseminating his thoughts. He has tweeted: "My use of social media is not presidential—it's MODERN DAY PRESIDENTIAL" (Trump, 2017). Twitter was a prominent strategy of his campaign. The ability to communicate directly with the public without interpretation (or fact-checking) by traditional media was apparently an effective tactic. Smyth (2016) described the 2016 presidential election and campaign as the first "social media election," and although Bernie Sanders used social media to organize many volunteers, Trump is "the master of Twitter" who "epitomizes" the social media presence in politics. The outsize influence of social media on the 2016 election led to a campaign that "descended to a level of incivility, of pandering to racism and ignorance, and downright lies that has no parallel in modern US politics" (Smyth, 2016). Now the sitting president, Trump continues to use Twitter to berate anyone who opposes him, to send messages (and threats) to foreign leaders, and to fire up his base, apparently to great effect.

> "The outsize influence of social media on the 2016 election led to a campaign that 'descended to a level of incivility, of pandering to racism and ignorance, and downright lies that has no parallel in modern US politics'" (Smyth, 2016).

In the first year of his tenure, Trump tweeted 2,568 times (including retweets), or 7+ times every day, to his approximately 63 million followers. Among those tweets are many that are controversial at best and insulting and intimidating at worst. According to Krieg (2018), Trump had insulted or used pejorative terms about close to 100 individuals. Of those he attacked, 75 were men (62 of whom were White) and 22 women (6 of whom were not White). Sometimes in response to a disparaging feed, other politicians enter the fray, so there are now many high-status politicians who engage in digital aggression and retaliation.

Trump has also shared anti-Muslim videos posted by a British far-right group and has used demeaning and derogatory words in tweets to Hillary Clinton, LaVar Ball, Kim Jong-un, Meryl Streep, Arnold Schwarzenegger, Whoopi Goldberg, Macy's, Ted Cruz, Mika Brzezinski, Robert De Niro, the cast of the popular Broadway show Hamilton, football players, his own original secretary of state, his attorney general, legislators in Congress, and foreign dignitaries. Some of these have responded in kind (on Twitter) with aggressive comments of their own.

Why does this matter? Consider this: I don't follow Donald Trump on Twitter, so one might think I am not affected by the content or tone of his tweets. But following him is only one way to see these tweets. A Gallup poll found that though only 8% of Americans follow him on Twitter (and only 4% read those regularly), 76% are aware of his tweets via other sources (Newport, 2018). When someone is the leader of the country, his tweets appear in every other media—on news websites, other social media, television news, and print news. The more outrageous and damaging the tweet, the more attention it gets. So, what we are seeing is the president of the United States engaging in both digital aggression and cyberbullying, with no apparent negative consequences. Yes, many are critical of his comments, but he gets more attention as a result. It does not change his behavior. However, it likely influences the behavior of others.

Roose (2018) claimed that social media has been "Trumpified"; political candidates at even local levels have been imitating Trump's hostile posture on Twitter, and have taken to creating disparaging nicknames for opponents, à la Trump. Interestingly, Roose pointed out that "anger travels further online than inspirational messages." The algorithms on social media platforms respond to the number of comments, and angry items get more attention. It's a sad commentary that in today's political and digital climate, the way to get noticed is to be obnoxious and aggressive. Taking his cue from Trump, Ben Kalasho, a city councilman is El Cajon, California, described social media as a superpower and said that he was inspired by how Trump used Twitter for political gain. Kalasho's posts were contentious and argumentative, because he had discovered that the more argumentative topics got more attention. As a postscript to this incident, this politician's use of Facebook resulted in a lawsuit in which Kalasho was accused of impeding "a man's free speech by blocking his comments on the councilmember's official Facebook page." He settled the lawsuit and resigned from his position in March 2019 (Avitabile, 2019).

Mary Anne Franks, a law professor and member of Twitter's Trust and Safety Council said, "The concern was that Mr. Trump, as the President, was using Twitter in such a manner, it encouraged and emboldened others to do the same." "You have children seeing the President of the US talking like this then they will think that is the way to talk. I don't think we'll see the full impact of this for many decades" (Buncombe, 2018). An illustration of the influence of Trump's behavior is his tweet in which he misspelled the name of congressional representative Schiff (spelled as Schitt). A Twitter post shortly thereafter said, "Just want to point out all the kids in school with the last name #Schiff getting bullied and name called #Schitt today because of the president of the US. I know because my nieces are Schiffs. #BeBest" (David, 2018). That tweet received 1,100 comments, 11,556 retweets, and 35,740 likes. A perusal of those comments shows that almost all are in support of the poster, and critical of Trump.

A fascinating study conducted by researchers Huang and Cornell (2019) documented the impact on the bullying behavior of middle school youth following the presidential election of 2016. These researchers have collected data in Virginia for many years, so they had a basis for comparison. In 2013 and 2015 surveys, there were no significant differences in the rates of teasing and bullying between Republican and Democratic districts. In 2017, however, both behaviors were significantly more prevalent (18% higher) in districts in which Trump had received the most votes compared to those in which Clinton prevailed. In Republican districts, teasing about race or ethnicity was 9% higher than in Democratic districts. Although these researchers did not enquire about the use of social media, we do know that middle school students are highly engaged with social media. There is no evidence to conclude that social media was an influence in the increase in bullying behaviors. However, consistent with the confirmation bias discussed later, it is conceivable that youth and their parents in Republican districts paid attention the aggressive tweets of Trump and other famous adults; it would be interesting to know whether this might account for the discrepancies in the behaviors.

Another study, using data from the FBI, Twitter, and U.S. Census data, examined the relationship between Trump's anti-Muslim tweets and hate crimes directed at Muslims (Müller & Schwarz, 2018). With meticulous analyses, the authors found that there was an increase in hate crimes directed at Muslims in counties that had high levels of Twitter usage during Trump's campaign. The researchers controlled for other factors that might affect the rate of hate crimes. They detected a strong correlation between Trump's tweets on Muslim-related themes and the number of hate crimes toward Muslims committed in high-Twitter-use districts. The authors examined the same dates (between the November election and the end of the year) for the Clinton, Bush, Obama, and Trump presidencies to compare the rates of anti-Muslim hate crimes. Prior to Trump's election, the largest increase in hate crimes occurred in that period after the 9/11 attacks on the World Trade Center. However, the spike in such events after Trump's election was significantly greater than that. Furthermore, the data showed that when Trump's tweets contained content derogatory toward Hispanics, ethnicity-based hate crimes increased. This study is important because of the multiple sources of data and the careful analysis, exemplifying the serious consequences of presidential cyberbullying or digital aggression.

To provide a theoretical and psychological basis for understanding this behavior, I reviewed the most prominent theories of aggression in Chapter 2. Those theories provide a basic understanding of aggression as a human behavior. Here, I look more specifically at components of those theories that might illuminate the psychology of the cyberaggression we are concerned about.

SOCIAL NORMING

There are several psychological processes that underscore the impact of high-status individuals (politicians, leaders, professional athletes, celebrities) engaging in these behaviors. The phenomenon of *social norming* has been studied by Schultz, Nolan, Cialdini, Goldstein, and Griskevicius (2007) with respect to a variety of behaviors (e.g., energy consumption, smoking, drinking). Individuals tend to behave in ways they believe is normative in the population. That is, behaviors are influenced by what a person *thinks* others consider to be desirable or acceptable or in accordance with perceived social norms. A person who thinks others will disapprove of their behavior is less likely to engage in that behavior, because social approval is valued. Of course, the individual weighs his or her behavior against a relevant reference group. For example, the college student will be influenced by the perception of the behavior of other college students, politicians by other politicians, the religious individual to other devout worshippers, and so forth. Conversely, if someone believes that most people engage in a given behavior, people are more likely to do so. A related psychological process that has been demonstrated in a variety of studies is that individuals tend to overestimate the prevalence of negative behaviors and underestimate that of positive ones and that they tend to be unaware of the extent they are influenced by these social norms (Cialdini, 2007).

This psychological understanding has been applied to practical situations—efforts to reduce undesirable or harmful behaviors (excessive drinking, not using seatbelts, etc.) by providing actual data about normative behavior. For example, to reduce harm from underage and excessive alcohol consumption in college students, some harm reduction programs for colleges publicize the data on average number of drinks consumed by students at their university (which is lower than students think they are). An experiment with five middle schools found that using posters to disseminate the data from anonymous school surveys was associated with reductions in bullying, victimization, attitudes that supported bullying (Perkins, Craig, & Perkins, 2011). Another study focused on an online petition site for debate about public issues, and found that "firestorms"—large amounts of angry, demeaning, profane comments directed toward a group—represented 20% of all comments on the site and had at least one aggressive element; in 9% there were two or more. These comments were interpreted by the authors as enforcing social norms, calling out those who they believed had violated implicit expectations of behavior. That is, when the target of these comments had violated a social norm, these legions of others took to the social media site to ensure their transgression was known. Interestingly, only 29.2% of commenters chose to be anonymous. The researchers reasoned that those whose motives for commenting were about promoting higher values (social justice, fairness, saving the environment, etc.) want to have their views known, and believe that including their names enhances their credibility.

So, what does this have to do with the cyberaggression and cyberbullying of prominent persons? It is reasonable to assume that with the barrage of tweets from Donald Trump and the increased use of social media by other politicians to criticize (or attack) their opponents, the perception for many people is that this behavior is commonplace and acceptable. Given that perceptions drive behavior, it is certainly possible that people who engage in cyberaggression see their behavior is within the normal range. Müller and Schwarz (2018) interpret their findings to say, "Trump's presidential campaign aided an unraveling of social norms that made people more willing to express views that were previously deemed socially unacceptable" (p. 3).

In a very interesting set of studies, Polish researchers found that frequent exposure to hate speech *desensitizes* people so that they no longer react negatively toward the hateful content or messages (Soral, Bilewicz, & Winlewski, 2018). They also increase their discriminatory behavior toward the group that has been repeatedly attacked with hate speech. A low level of sensitivity to hate speech led to more prejudiced beliefs and attitudes toward the target of the hate speech. These studies confirmed the role of desensitization (or a lower sensitivity, after repeated exposure to hate speech) in creating a perception that this is normative behavior. Repeated exposure to negative content can revise social norms through the mechanism of desensitization. Thus, the repeated tweets of the president with derogatory messages (e.g., the news media are all fake news, his attorney general is incompetent, Hillary Clinton is a criminal, the Mueller investigation is a witch hunt) serve, for a segment of the population, to desensitize the audience so that these messages seem less objectionable and eventually seem to be the norm.

MODELING

In addition to social norming, concepts from social learning theory, discussed in Chapter 2, help to explain why the cyberaggression and cyberbullying perpetrated by Trump is so harmful. Social learning theory was first proposed by Albert Bandura (1973). The influence of *modeling* of aggression was an important focus of his work. I expand here on the role of modeling in learning and maintaining behavior. Bandura pointed out that learning via observation of others is quite efficient, as we don't have to experience every possible (and perhaps fatal) outcome of a behavior to learn it. By observing others' behavior, and the outcome of those behaviors, one can acquire the behaviors that have positive outcomes. That is, the learner experiences vicarious reinforcement when the model is rewarded for the behavior, and when the outcome is not reinforced or is punished, the learner or observer can determine that the behavior may not be one to add to his or her repertoire. The individual creates cognitive models (mental images) of these behaviors that are stored in the brain for future use.

Some characteristics of the model are important and apply to the current situation. People are more likely to imitate the behavior of people they see as similar to themselves. Trump's portrayal as the "non-politician" and champion of the American worker was effective in creating a persona people could relate to and identify with. More alarming, however, is his espousal of racist and xenophobic beliefs that resonate with people who share those biases and have previously been harshly judged for those ideas. Although he, too, has been sharply criticized for these views, he knows that those who will vote for him and who come to his raucous rallies see themselves in him, and model their rhetoric after his. Learners note what happens to the model who exhibits a behavior, and what his supporters see is that he was elected president of the most powerful country in the world, is extremely wealthy, has a beautiful wife, and appears unconstrained by protocol or established procedures for that office.

Bandura (1977) reiterated his ideas regarding the modeling of aggressive behavior. He noted that aggressive models increase the level of aggression in observers; models who show restrained and nonaggressive behavior also influence behavior of others. However, all models are not equally effective at influencing the behavior of observers. In general, people who serve as influential role models have notable assets, among which high social status and power are most salient. The position of president of the United States is the epitome of status and power, conferring considerable weight on his function as a model. The consequences of the observed aggressive behavior indicate whether the behavior is likely to bring benefits or liabilities should the observer imitate the behavior. The fact that Trump appears to engage in his aggressive behavior (particularly though not exclusively on social media) without negative consequences increases the likelihood of his behavior being enacted by observers. The implicit message is that when such behavior goes unpunished and uncensored, the behavior is acceptable. This frees the observer of any inhibitions toward using social media in an aggressive manner.

During the 2017–2018 academic year, following Trump's election, more than 50 incidents in 26 states were reported in which a White student taunted a minority peer with racially themed epithets either referring to Trump explicitly or using his words (Samaha, Hayes, & Ansari, 2017). Many of the 54 cases investigated by these reporters were directed at Latinx students, who were subjected to chants of "Build that wall" or told they would be deported. Several parents reported that their children were afraid to go to school after such incidents. When school districts took a stand against speech that caused some students to feel unsafe (having assemblies, sending e-mails, promoting multicultural understanding), it was not without backlash. The challenge, some school administrators said, was that the "build the wall" phrase was used by the president of the country, and it is difficult to discipline children who say the same thing. One example is from a high school in North Carolina, where a student's yearbook quote "build that wall" resulted in the confiscation of the yearbooks by the school. The school explained (via Facebook) that the post was "inappropriate." There were many comments, including one that said, "Quoting the POTUS is never inappropriate." Here again, young people are modeling their behavior upon that of the most powerful person in the country, and do not recognize (or care about) the impact of their behavior on their classmates.

CONFIRMATION BIAS

One other psychological phenomenon is relevant to this discussion. *Confirmation bias* refers to the tendency to seek information that confirms what we already believe, and to discount or disregard information that contradicts these beliefs. This phenomenon was discussed as early as the 17th century and applied in a psychological context in the early 20th century (Nickerson, 1998). When supporters of Trump hear or read about his tweets, it is likely that they respond positively because the message confirms their previous positive opinion of him and his platform. The repetition is likely to strengthen their conviction. They also likely avoid or discount messages or information that counters those messages.

Of course, there are other influential models that engage in digital aggression—celebrities, athletes, and others in the limelight. The focus in this chapter has been on Trump because he holds the position of highest status and power, and by virtue of that status, has perhaps outsized influence. Other celebrities have considerable influence as well; they too may be more digitally aggressive when Trump models that behavior, and their fans follow suit. Followers may feel emboldened to say things in social media or otherwise that would have been unacceptable just a few years ago. People may have held private opinions about various groups (e.g., racial or ethnic minorities, immigrants, LGBT persons), but to outwardly speak of them in pejorative and aggressive terms was a violation of social norms. It appears that those norms have changed in response to the modeling by the cyberbully in chief.

MORAL DISENGAGEMENT

Moral disengagement is a cognitive process (Bandura, 1976, 1999, 2002, 2017; Bandura, Barbaranelli, Caprara, & Pastorelli, 1996) by which people justify their immoral behavior to themselves and others so that they do not feel guilty about what they have done. People (with the exception of the few with serious psychopathology) develop internal standards of right and wrong, and endeavor to act in ways that are consistent with those standards. If they do not, they typically feel guilt and shame about their actions, and these are unpleasant enough that most seek to avoid those feelings. However, many examples from history reveal that people also behave in ways that are clearly violations of commonly accepted values. Here are the mechanisms that may be employed to justify or rationalize such behavior.

Moral justification is the thought that the behavior is serving a higher purpose—it is the means to a just end. Torture of prisoners has been justified as necessary for the safety of the populace. The use of the atomic bomb in World War II was justified as necessary to end the war quickly and save lives. Donald Trump might tell himself that his Twitter rants are needed to alert the citizenry to important information, since the "fake news" cannot be relied upon to do so. Similarly, *advantageous comparison* refers to minimizing one's misdeeds by telling oneself they are not as bad as a more severe action. A person who demeans another with words, calling them names and spreading untrue rumors, can tell themselves that that's not as bad as hurting them physically. When there are many people involved in an action, people convince themselves that no one else did anything, and they were just one small cog in a large machine (*responsibility diffusion*). A bystander to a school bully who does not intervene can point to the other bystanders who did nothing either. A concerned citizen who chooses not to participate in a protest march against a policy that he or she believes is wrong can rationalize that there were so many people there and his or her presence would not matter. It is also possible to blame others for one's immoral acts, using the mechanism of *displacement of responsibility*. For example, a person who steals a necessity from a store may rationalize that stealing was necessary only because the store overcharged customers, making such items unaffordable. *Distortion of consequences* can reduce guilt by minimizing the consequences of one's immoral act; that is, it really didn't hurt anyone, or it was just a trifling amount. One of the most insidious cognitive ploys is that of *dehumanization.* We excuse our behavior by portraying the target as something other than human, something lacking human emotions and desires. Referring to human beings as animals, for example, "pigs" or "dogs" (as Trump has done often), is a common way of justifying inhuman treatment. Trump's justification about this penchant for dehumanizing anyone who opposes him is that "the big problem, this country has is being politically correct" (Bump, 2018).

Social ecological theory reminds us that cyberbullies do not emerge in a vacuum. The chronosystem is the necessary context—a world in which digital media predominate and individuals are nearly universally connected to digital devices. The macrosystem with our cultural values is relevant as well, and it is disturbing to think that hostility and incivility has become acceptable or at least tolerated. If we emulate public figures and celebrities, and extol the virtues of freedom of speech, it is difficult to persuade the public that such behavior is inconsistent with our democratic values. The larger institutions, including the economy and education, are influenced by those outer circles, and the call for educators to teach critical thinking as an essential life skill meets opposition from groups who believe schools should restrict their teaching to "academics."

SUMMARY

In this chapter, I described various psychological mechanisms by which Trump's aggressive behavior in cyberspace has had enormous influence on the tone and norms of discourse on social media and other digital platforms. It will be difficult to counteract the effect of such a powerful person who is the epitome of a cyberbully. The behavior is positively reinforced by attention and the acclaim and adoration from his supporters. I hope that his targets would not be goaded into responding in kind, further contributing to social norms that are destructive to civil society. I also hope that readers will endeavor to express their opinions; disagree with others, in a respectful manner that does not devolve into ad hominem attacks; and provide alternative models for online debate. In my case, I hide the social media posts of people who are consistently aggressive, which keeps my exposure to the venom to a minimum. I cannot avoid the news report of Trump's latest tweetstorm, but I can choose to stop at the headline.

Krista Millay's Story

The Women's Resource Center (WRC) at the university is dedicated to combatting sexism and misogyny and to preventing sexual assault. The Center offers workshops and trainings on sexual assault prevention to groups on campus as part of its outreach efforts. The center works to create a campus environment that is welcoming for all members of the campus community.

Also on campus are "Greek" organizations (fraternities and sororities whose names are Greek letters) that are local chapters of national groups. Most of these have large houses where meetings and events are held and where members often reside. The 2015 data on the University of Arizona from the AAU Campus Climate Survey on Sexual Assault and Misconduct showed that a significant portion of sexual assaults on the campus occurred in the houses of Greek organizations (Millay, 2017).

Fraternities and sororities are expected to take up charitable causes. In 2016, shortly after the presidential election, one of the fraternities, ΑΕΠ (AEPi), organized a "Walk a Mile in Her Shoes" event at the University of Arizona. This nation-wide event features fraternity members walking a mile wearing red, high heeled shoes. The stated intent is to increase awareness of sexual violence toward women in a "playful" way (https://www.walkamileinhershoes.org/).

A member of the fraternity telephoned the WRC less than a week before the event was scheduled and requested WRC's support. Krista Millay, director of the WRC at the time, spoke to the student and declined to support the event, explaining that the "playful" nature of the event was inconsistent with the WRC view of sexism and sexual assault as very serious matters. She also noted that the event demeaned transgender and nonbinary members of the university and community. The student was disappointed and called back later in the day to enquire whether the WRC would protest the event; Millay explained that the WRC would not do so. She had no further contact of any kind with the student or other representative of the fraternity.

One would think that refusal would settle the matter, but alas, it did not end there. The Dean of Students Office soon received a telephone call from the student's father, and Millay had a call from a high school employer of the student, both attempting to influence Millay to change her decision. She did not. The fraternity cancelled the event.

Several days later, a "news" article appeared on https://totalfratmove.com/. (A quick visit to the site will show the reader how ironic is its antisexual assault claim, and the sort of "news" that it publishes.) The article included false information that was fabricated to paint the WRC, and Millay in particular, as the unreasonable obstacle to a noble cause. The so-called news included an e-mail exchange between Millay and the student in which Millay was quite insulting and rude. However, that e-mail exchange never took place. The person who wrote the story never contacted Millay to verify the information, nor did he take any steps to authenticate the bogus e-mail exchange. A brief perusal of the website—which caters to fraternity members—makes it clear that its "news" is not an example of responsible journalism.

Once the story was online, the harassment began. Despite the rather narrow audience of the website, enough of the viewers were incensed by the false story that they chose to attack Millay by sending hateful e-mails, voicemails, and mail (as a university employee, her e-mail and phone number were easy to find) and posting negative comments on Facebook. These hateful responses were not just from fraternity members, but from students and administrators of other universities, mothers, fathers, doctors, and lawyers. They criticized her for being too concerned with being "politically correct" and "feminist," and made many scurrilous and insulting remarks. She received disgusting photos and pornographic images, and people stated that they would seek her termination. Millay created a standard response to such e-mails that noted the article's falsehoods and included some data about sexual assault in an effort to educate these individuals. Only 3 of more than 100 attackers responded to her e-mail acknowledging that their attacks were based on incomplete information at best.

Being targeted by such hateful attacks took its emotional toll on Millay. The unexpected barrage of pernicious messages created tension in important relationships; it is hard for others to understand how an experience like this can overwhelm the target.

Millay filed a complaint regarding the student, whose behavior violated the student code of conduct. To her knowledge, he was called in to the dean's office for a conversation, but no sanctions were imposed. This is a disappointing response, or lack thereof. The false information that was promulgated caused a deluge of digital aggression toward Millay, whose "offense" was to take a stand and make decisions based on the best principles of sexual assault prevention. She expected a stronger action, and perhaps a public statement, from the university administration, making it clear that social media should not be used by students to disseminate false information. Millay ultimately left the university.

The story was covered in the local newspaper (https://tucson.com/news/local/fake-news-story-leads-to-harassment-of-university-of-arizona/article_9627dd68-f692-51f5-bdd5-b6772fa1393e.html) and the student news paper (http://www.wildcat.arizona.edu/article/2017/04/total-frat-move-and-greek-life-culture), explaining the events and the misinformation and outright lies that were included on the website. Several months later, Millay wrote an OpEd that was published on the everydayfeminism.com (https://everydayfeminism.com/2017/06/fraternity-men-need-to-do-more/) website. It included specific and practical steps that fraternity members could take if they really wanted to take action against sexual assault. The OpEd was shared 676 times on Facebook, and we can only hope that ultimately the message reached the intended audience.

The incident highlights how easy it is to disseminate false information online, and how many readers consume "information," without taking the time to consider the source or check facts. And, as in many of these stories, the disinhibited responses appear to be out of proportion to the situation, perhaps confirming that many rants and attacks are related to underlying anger and dissatisfaction rather than reasoned disagreement with someone's ideas.

4

Online Disinhibition Effect

The sheer volume of digital aggression is a challenge for people to understand, and the psychological theories summarized in Chapters 2 and 3 have been offered as possible clues. The theory of *online disinhibition* is often referred to as the explanation of the cruelty often seen online, and because it is so frequently mentioned, I will devote this chapter to looking closely at it. Although some of the tenets of the theory may be a bit esoteric, I make my best effort at making the ideas understandable.

Disinhibition as a psychological concept was known long before the internet and is a symptom of several mental disorders, including *mania, chronic alcohol abuse,* and *borderline personality disorder.* Disinhibition means a reduced ability to control (inhibit) impulses that are inappropriate or in violation of social norms. If I am tempted to steal an item from the store, I remind myself this is both wrong and illegal, and I inhibit that impulse. If I stole it anyway, that would be an example of disinhibition. When observers noticed a similar behavior on the internet, the term was adapted and called *online disinhibition.* In this chapter, after defining the term, I review the essential components of this theory, and then examine some of the research that has tested it. Finally, I discuss

> *Disinhibition* as a psychological concept was known long before the internet and is a symptom of several mental disorders, including *mania, chronic alcohol abuse,* and *borderline personality disorder.*

its relevance to the concerns about the increase in prevalence and intensity of online aggression.

A basic definition of *online disinhibition* is "a psychological state in which individuals feel less inhibited in the online environment" (Cheung, Wong, & Chan, 2016). It is a state in which the usual internal censors (conscience) are ignored or silenced so that aggressive and other socially inappropriate behaviors that would not be exhibited in the offline world are unleashed. Joinson (2007) focused his discussion on two common ways online disinhibition is apparent: in online communications: "flaming" and personal self-disclosure, and viewing online pornography. He provided experimental evidence that personal and even intimate self-disclosure occurred more often in online than in face-to-face interactions, and that the same was true for flaming (aggressive, argumentative) behaviors. It appears that people's reluctance to be expressive toward others, in both positive and negative ways, is reduced in a digital environment. Accessing online pornography is attributed largely to the ability to hide one's online activities from others to diminish the associated shame of discovery.

Lapidot-Lefler and Barak (2012) contend that anonymity is the primary driver of online disinhibition. They describe early research by Zimbardo and others that found increases in aggressive behaviors when study participants are anonymous.[1] They speculate that being anonymous implies a lack of accountability that allows some people to feel free to act aggressively without fear of repercussions. These authors also point out that not all studies have found clear evidence that anonymity directly influences online disinhibition. Other researchers (e.g., Vogeser, Singh, & Góritz, 2018) disagree with the emphasis on anonymity and note that considerable online disinhibition occurs in non-anonymous digital platforms. In a study of online hate websites, the anonymity of the creator of the content was investigated along with other factors. Results revealed that there was no effect for identifiability; that is, the degree to which violence and conflict were promoted on the site was not associated with whether or not the author was known or anonymous. Donald Trump appears to be quite disinhibited online, although this is not a departure from his offline rhetoric.

John Suler's (2004, 2005, 2016) theory of the *online disinhibition effect* was an early effort to understand the unique ways in which people interact online. Published in 2004, it was cited almost 3,064 times (as of March 2019) in subsequent scholarly publications and is often referred to in the popular media. Because of its significant influence, it is important that we scrutinize it closely. Readers are familiar with the basic premise of the theory: People often behave differently online (or using digital devices) than they do offline. While this is what Suler proposed, it is an oversimplification. Joinson (1998, 2007) has also written about this phenomenon and on occasion disagrees with Suler's interpretation, as noted later.

THE THEORY

Before we delve more deeply into Suler's ideas, there are several caveats that must be acknowledged. First, the theory was developed prior to the explosion of social media, which are the loci of much disinhibited behavior. Second, the theory is based on the psychoanalytic theoretical lens, which emphasizes unconscious processes. Third, the online disinhibition effect does not affect all internet users in the same way, nor does it even apply to every platform an individual uses. That is, it is far from a universal phenomenon. Fourth, Suler describes two types of online inhibition—benign inhibition and toxic inhibition. We focus here on toxic inhibition. Finally, the theory has yet to produce robust empirical evidence of its influence on online behavior.

The online disinhibition effect refers to people's behavior when ordinary social norms and rules are abandoned in an environment (the digital universe) where fear of the judgment of others is also suspended. In offline life, most of us inhibit our antisocial (or inappropriate) impulses because we are aware that acting upon them is socially inappropriate, and we don't want others to judge us harshly. We tend to abide by social norms. In digital spaces, it seems those constraints are less salient, and people sometimes behave in ways that discount their concerns about how their behavior aligns with their social code or how others might judge their behavior. This is online disinhibition. Toxic disinhibition applies when the disinhibited behavior is angry, aggressive, vulgar, threatening, directed toward others. Joinson (2007) points to experimental evidence of both toxic and benign disinhibition, but these studies were conducted prior to the widespread use of social media, with small samples, in analog situations.

Suler (2016) makes an interesting observation that, while it does not figure prominently in his theory, is quite germane to the discussion. That is, social norms in the digital world vary widely from one platform to another. There are some groups or sites where vulgar language and extreme rants are typical—thus normative—whereas if the same comments were posted on other platforms, they would be considered shocking and most likely would be reported. Thus, if one visits a variety of sites with varying norms, one could easily lose sight of what type of communication is acceptable on which platform.

The online disinhibition effect is widely observed. What Suler and other theorists attempt is to understand *how* and *why* that behavior emerges. Suler (2016) considers that the psychological (and psychoanalytical) process of *regression*—a return to earlier developmental stages—is one explanation for the disinhibited behaviors. He claims that *toxic* disinhibition can be seen as a "developmentally immature catharsis of primitive impulses" (p. 97). That is, when someone releases pent-up unconscious and often diffuse anger or other strong emotion via digital means, it may appear as a harsh comment that might have been stated more judiciously in an offline conversation, or it may take the form of an angry rant directed toward those with different opinions.

Now to the meat of Suler's theory. He originally (Suler, 2004) proposed six factors that facilitate toxic online disinhibition but added two more in 2016. The first of these is *dissociative anonymity*. People often think it is anonymity alone that encourages toxic disinhibition, but many egregious digital attacks are perpetrated by non-anonymous individuals. *Dissociation* is a process of separating the self psychologically from one's surroundings. While it can be a symptom of mental illness, most of us have found ourselves driving past our destination without realizing it or daydreaming during a class and being suddenly returned to the present when our name was called by the instructor. These are common dissociative experiences and are not indicative of any psychological disturbance.

So, it is not just anonymity but perhaps specific aspects of anonymity that account for the loosening of internal restraints. Dissociative anonymity is a consequence of being unknown to our contacts online. They may know some details about us that we choose to provide, but those may not either completely or accurately portray our identities. Furthermore, the dissociative process allows the individual to see the digital persona as separate from the offline self. This sense of our online self being detached from our offline or usual self while also feeling unknown to our online audience is what encourages the toxic disinhibition. In other words, it is not our everyday self that is disinhibited, but it is our digital self, a separate identity whose behavior we are not responsible for. Multiple personality disorder is an extreme and pathological version of the existence of multiple selves.

The next factor is *deindividuation*. This is not a new concept (Gustave Le Bon discussed it in 1905; Suler, 2016) but is one that Suler incorporated into his theory. It is also related to anonymity, in that it refers to what happens in a crowd or large group when one's self-awareness diminishes and one's identity as a member of the group predominates. A person feels less responsible for their individual actions because they are merely part of the group. The other feature of this "crowd mentality" is that one does not see the targets or readers of offensive posts as individuals, but as part of a nameless, featureless audience. That encourages deindividuation. Joinson (2007) questions whether deindividuation is as central to online disinhibition as Suler (2004) suggested. Joinson proposes that it may be that the online context has different social norms and that users enact a social identity consistent with that context.

Several researchers have pointed to the social identity model of deindividuation effects (SIDE) as a useful framework (see Reicher, Spears, & Postmes, 1995) to understand the impact of deindividuation. This theory not only addresses the phenomenon of deindividuation but also contributes to our understanding of the high degree of polarization seen in some online platforms or communities. SIDE was in some ways a reaction to the notion of deindividuation as described earlier. Its proponents disagreed with the notion that people in a crowd lose self-awareness and thus become disinhibited. The SIDE model (Spears, 2017) posits that in the group situation, when individuals are anonymous, social identities and norms are dominant, so that the individual is likely to conform to the social norms of the group, which in some cases is supportive of aggressive and hostile discourse. The model suggests that the process called *deindividuation* by Joinson and Suler is more accurately described as *depersonalization*, which means the individual identities are subsumed by the group identity. People see others in the group (and are seen by them) as an exemplar of the group identity rather than as individuals with unique characteristics and opinions. Spears (2017) notes that several empirical studies (in labs, not in vivo) have supported the hypothesis that depersonalization leads to stronger group identity and adherence to group norms. Furthermore, adherence to group norms, and the concomitant importance of clarifying distinctions between groups, leads to more polarized positions than might otherwise develop.

A related factor is that of *invisibility.* Until recently, when livestreaming is possible on several social media platforms, other users could not see individual users in real time, and the knowledge of this contributes to thinking that one's behaviors—especially those that are unacceptable—will not be noticed. On sites where user's identities are known, being visually unobservable means there is no way to notice if others are signaling disapproval with facial expressions or even making sounds of objection. Suler (2016) reminds us that the classic psychoanalytic office arrangement has the analyst seated so that he or she is not visible to the patient because this encourages disinhibited stream-of-consciousness content that is central to the psychoanalytic process. Research to be cited later in this chapter examines the importance of lack of eye contact in this realm.

Much social media interaction and other digital activities are *asynchronous.* That means that once a message, image, comment, and others is posted, a response occurs only after a lapse in time. That lapse could be seconds, but is generally minutes, hours, or days later. Suler (2016) contends that the absence of feedback in real time may mean one is unaware of the inappropriateness of the post quickly enough to modify and comply with social norms. He also suggests that when one must wait for a response, rumination is fostered, which may promote more self-disclosure. That absence of synchronicity provides an opportunity to "hit and run." One can express one's thoughts or opinions and exit the site without having to contend with any comments or criticisms. Of course, the other side of asynchronicity is that users could carefully compose their posts and the like without feeling pressure to respond instantaneously. This should lead to more thoughtful, relevant, and carefully composed messages.

Solipsistic introjection is a psychoanalytic mechanism that involves incorporating another's thoughts or ideas without analyzing or deconstructing them. The developing child introjects the moral values instilled by the parents, for example. When we read text online or on phone screens, we hear the words in our minds as our own voice, making it easier to introject the ideas. We also tend to expand the voice into a character in our minds that is based partly on the messages and other known information, but also includes our own imagination, expectations, and needs. Suler (2016) explains that we imbue these created characters with characteristics of significant others in our lives, leading to *transference,* or experiencing emotional reactions that are remnants of those important relationships. He says, "Solipsistic introjection operates when people experience their posts as a kind of disinhibited murmuring to themselves, with seemingly no one listening" (p. 103).

Online gaming, in which players create a character (often in the form of an avatar), may contribute to a state of *dissociative imagination.* In other words, people invest psychic energy in their online characters and see them as existing in a parallel universe, which they can leave and return to their offline self. For individuals of marginal stability, the two "realities" may blur, and they may have difficulty distinguishing experiences online from their daily lives, experiencing online events (disappointments, friendships, etc.) as though they are a central part of their world.

Suler (2016) next focused on *perceived privacy,* in which, despite intellectually understanding that anything we post online can be retrieved, copied, saved, stored, and used for marketing and other purposes, we tend to subconsciously think that our online life is in fact private. After all, we routinely enter credit card numbers and other personal data when making online purchases. Even though these sites encrypt the information, protecting it more effectively, there is always a chance that data can be retrieved for nefarious purposes. There have been news reports of databases from large corporations being hacked and the personal data stolen. Even a site like Snapchat, where users see posts disappear quickly, has been hacked and "disappeared" posts made available. Furthermore, other users can quickly take screenshots of another's post and can circulate that even when the original post is gone. This became a major issue when on March 15, 2019, 50 Muslims were murdered in New Zealand and the incident streamed online by the perpetrator. Although social media sites removed the video, it was copied many times and continued to be available and recirculated after the site took it down.

Because many of the accoutrements that convey status and authority are not always apparent online, *attenuated status* and *authority* allows some people to be more honest and forthright in online settings. Suler (2016) ascribes this to *net democracy* or the sense that in cyberspace, equality is assumed. Because we are less likely to fear judgment or rebuke from peers, online disinhibition may emerge. Joinson interprets this factor as the result of *reduced social cues*. He notes that there are digital social cues (e.g., emojis), but they are not equivalent to those in a face-to-face interaction. We must keep in mind that the expansion of social media, the use of video and/or livestreaming, may reduce the effect of those factors.

Finally, Suler (2016) describes the influence of *social facilitation* on online disinhibition. In some social media platforms, those who display online behaviors that are aggressive or offensive may be rewarded with encouragement or approval from others who frequent that online space. Visitors to the site might observe aggressive language and images, and identify with the aggressor (a psychoanalytic process). This is also consistent with social learning theory; Trump's supporters frequently laud his tweets when they attack others. Not only is he rewarded with their approval, but others who observe these interactions are also affected by this social facilitation. Furthermore, when there are numerous people who observe the bad behavior and do not oppose it, the result may be that the individual observer thinks "If no one else objects, why should I take a chance on being censored for doing so?"

Joinson (2007) mentions several factors that Suler (2016) did not. Self-awareness may be *private* (turned inward) or *public* (toward the environment). Public self-awareness takes precedence when the individual is being judged or evaluated or when they are conspicuous in some way (different from others in a group). Some theorists believe that when private self-awareness is increased, people are more likely to self-disclose and may not attend to environmental cues about what is appropriate. He criticizes research that tested this hypothesis because of the nature of the experimental manipulations. Joinson also conducted studies on the role of self-awareness and generally supported the importance of the focus of self-awareness on online behavior and the degree of disinhibition displayed.

Given all these mechanisms by which online disinhibition can be influential, the fact is that not everyone who is susceptible is affected. Suler (2016) argues that there are intrapersonal variables that interact with these influences that determine the outcome. From a psychoanalytic perspective, the more forceful the unconscious needs, the more likely the individual will express them in a disinhibited manner. He suggests that certain personality types are more susceptible to the effect; histrionic and narcissistic personalities are more prone to express themselves in any environment, so they are likely to be more disinhibited online as well. On the other hand, paranoid and compulsive people are often more guarded, and so they are less likely to be vulnerable to the online disinhibition effect. Personality traits "trust, extroversion, impulsivity, guilt, and shame all emerge as traits that modulate disinhibition" (p. 108), so that the interaction between individual variables and features of the online context ultimately drives the behaviors.

RESEARCH

Most of the research on online disinhibition is based on analog studies, those conducted in a laboratory under contrived conditions. Nevertheless, they suggest useful lines of inquiry.

The absence of eye contact has been implicated in the online disinhibition process. Lapidot-Lefler and Barak (2012) conducted an experiment where they manipulated anonymity, visibility, and eye contact in dyads drawn from 142 college student participants in Israel. The dyads were given a situation to discuss via online chat and instructed they must reach a consensus decision on the best outcome. The debate related to which member of the dyad would receive a medication that was needed to save the life of someone close to the participant. Anonymity was manipulated by either providing or withholding personal information about the participants, visibility was controlled by having a webcam that showed a side view of the participant, and eye contact involved having a webcam mounted at eye level and instructing participants to maintain eye contact. Transcripts of the chat interactions were assessed via expert ratings, analysis of the transcribed conversations, and participant self-report. The researchers calculated a "flaming" score for each dyad. Results demonstrated that flaming and threats were less frequent when participants had eye contact with their dyad partner, and in fact eye contact had a stronger effect on the disinhibition than did anonymity and invisibility.

Another study used a novel method in its experiment to assess the role of social cues in online disinhibition. Voggeser et al. (2018) conceptualize disinhibition as a lack of self-control and propose that online disinhibition is fostered by an absence of social cues in the digital context. Participants were 650 men and women recruited from Facebook and online forums. The researchers believed that *ego depletion* is a condition in which people have used up their self-control and are temporarily unable to access it.

This can occur when one is in a situation with multiple distractions and one has to expend considerable effort to maintain self-control, or when one is exhausted after a long work-day. It is also possible that some individuals are temperamentally less able to exert self-control or have a condition that interferes with that ability, such as chronic pain or a debilitating physical condition.

Voggeser et al. (2018) used the color Stroop test to simulate ego depletion. The participants were shown a word that named a color (e.g., red, green, blue, or yellow) presented on a screen and asked to name the color in which the word was printed. The words sometimes matched the color (i.e., the word *red* was printed in red) and sometimes did not (the word *red* is printed in green). There were 64 words; the depletion condition viewed 52 words that were incongruent (color and word) and 12 congruent, while the control group viewed 12 incongruent and 52 congruent words. The outcome was a variation on the Stroop task, in which the words were not color names but "emotional" words (either neutral, negative, or taboo (swear) words). Reaction times for the correctly identified colors were compared with each word type, with the expectation that longer times would be associated with taboo words. Immediately after completing the task, participants were briefly surveyed about the feelings toward the task and their overall mood.

The results were quite interesting. First, in the color Stroop test, participants were slower to respond to the incongruent words, as expected, and those in the experimental condition, who saw more incongruent trials, rated the task as more difficult than those who saw mostly congruent words. On the emotional Stroop task, there were no differences between the conditions on the ratings of difficulty or mood. On the emotional Stroop task, the depleted participants (the experimental group) did not respond at different speeds to the different word types, but participants the control group (undepleted) were the fastest at the neutral words, a bit slower to react to negative words, and significantly slower when viewing taboo words. Participants in the depleted condition were significantly faster responding to taboo words than those in the control condition. What this means is that depleted participants (those who had used up their self-control doing the more difficult color Stroop task) did not differentiate between the word types (which in this study were simulating "social cues"), but the undepleted participants did respond to the social cues by reacting differently to the word types.

RELEVANCE

The research reported previously is sparse, but intriguing. First, we need clear empirical evidence that the online disinhibition effects exist and can be measured. Second, we need more and larger studies to test the many hypotheses regarding influential factors that either encourage or curtail that effect. We also need to consider how individual differences in such variables as personality, age, gender, education, stress levels, and others interact with features of the digital environment to influence the degree of disinhibition observed. Finally, at some point, we need studies using actual versus simulated conditions to deepen our understanding of this phenomenon.

There is no question that there is a great deal of hateful, offensive, aggressive material that is transmitted via digital means. Online disinhibition has been proposed as an explanation for this behavior. We also need to consider what else might account for it. The theories in Chapter 2 may also illuminate the process, and while online disinhibition is frequently referenced, it should not obscure other potential explanations.

I believe it is unlikely that we will be able to dramatically reduce the amount of digital aggression that is enacted, but I do think as our understanding increases, we will be able to assist those who are targeted and perhaps diminish the psychological distress they experience. That is my strong hope.

SUMMARY

In this chapter, we looked closely at the theory of the online disinhibition effect. Although the phenomenon—many people appearing less inhibited or careful online—is often proposed as an explanation of the aggressive and hateful material some people post online, it is an understanding of how this works that is elusive. We looked at Suler's theory in some detail, and also looked at some of the research that has been done that is relevant. What we found is that despite the frequent citations and mentions of the online disinhibition effect, there is little if any conclusive evidence that the proposed psychological mechanisms involved are as proposed. These are complex processes that are not easy to measure, so we must be aware that this well-known theory has not yet been tested.

Adam Smith's Story

Adam Smith was not someone who regularly protested about social justice issues. In fact, the 2012 incident that dramatically affected his life was the very first time he had done such a thing. He was a business executive who was raised in a religious tradition that taught him that he was superior—to women, LGBT persons, and all those not part of the religious community. At the time of his experience of digital aggression, he had reached a point in his life when he began to question the teachings he had lived by, perhaps inspired by the coming-out of his brother-in-law. His brother-in-law declared his sexual homosexual orientation, and Adam observed how freeing that disclosure had been.

Adam was actively questioning his values and identity, reevaluating the worldview and beliefs he had previously accepted as true. He began to discuss his process of searching for his personal principles and philosophies with a few close family members, who were worried about these changes and the consequences. Coincidentally, at that time there was a call for people to protest the Chick-fil-A fast-food franchise, whose CEO had professed opposition to LGBT persons and opposed laws that permitted adoption by LGBTs. The idea behind the protest was that if many people went to the stores and requested a free cup of water, the company would be hurt financially.

Smith decided this was an opportunity to experiment with his newly acquired thinking that respected LGBT persons and all persons as equal. When he arrived at the drive-through window of the local restaurant, he got his cup of water, but went on to explain to the worker why the company was hateful, strongly chastised her for working there, and did not cease his harangue at her request. He recorded their interaction and posted it on YouTube, making his protest action a public one as well as a personal statement.

The response he received was unexpected and extreme. Smith was fired from his job as a CFO of a company; hate messages bombarded the company's phone lines and drew negative attention to the company. The comments on his video were almost unanimously critical, condemning, and shaming. His personal details (address, names of children, schools they attended) were made public, and he began to receive hate messages— by phone, by hand delivery to his mailbox, and finally the one that elevated fears for safety to an untenable degree. He felt he lost his identity and his reputation. These missives he received were not mildly worded criticisms. Messages were vengeful and vulgar, urged him to kill himself, said that he was against God, shamed him, said he did not deserve to be alive, and so on. One package delivered via the USPS contained feces. When someone nailed a hate letter to his door, which meant they had located and approached the Smith home (which did not have close neighbors) and did not fear discovery, Adam Smith feared for the safety of his family, and recognized that one of the haters could decide to do more than send messages.

He and his family left their home, first staying in a hotel and ultimately selling their house and purchasing an recreational vehicle or camper (RV). The incident plagued his job search, because companies routinely search the internet for information on potential executive employees, and he was seen as a risk. Although the fear of physical attacks diminished once the family left Tucson, it took several years to heal emotionally.

I asked Smith whether he has since boycotted social media. Although he did briefly do so, he now is back in cyberspace, using several platforms but primarily engaged with Facebook. His four children have a joint Facebook page that they share with only a few familiar people they know offline. The children do not have cell phones, although the eldest child, at 16, may be approaching the point at which Adam thinks he is ready.

The remarkable thing about Smith's story is that despite being "brought to [his] knees" by these events, he believes that he unconsciously chose this path to create the reasons to completely reset himself, to discover his inner truth, and find his way in the world. He has engaged in a difficult and courageous struggle to re-invent himself and to appreciate his more genuine self and his openness to opportunities and challenges that lead to growth.

Adam Smith's story is important for several reasons. First, Adam could be viewed as the aggressor in the initial incident. He filmed his interaction with the Chick-fil-A employee over her objections and then posted the video online. Although Smith did not set out to harm this employee—she represented the CEO whose views Smith was protesting—her privacy was violated. Very quickly, the tables were turned, and Smith became the target, and the severity of the attacks quickly escalated. It is perhaps illustrative of the dynamic of much digital aggression that aggressors tend to attract others to "gang up" on someone whose post or image or blog or whatever is the original stimulus. The group mentality, where new recruits are emboldened by the virulence of other attackers, occurs offline as well, but the huge audience online can make it seem as though one is universally despised. The other dynamic is that of the perpetrator becoming the target. It is not the exception that a digital attack is met with a counterattack, and an incident can "blow up" quickly and dramatically.

NOTE

1. Zimbardo had female subjects in his experiment dress to hide their identity (anonymous condition) or wear nametags. The subjects were told to give electric shocks to someone, and the anonymous participants were two times as willing to give the shocks as those who were not anonymous.

5

Online Personas

Who am I? is the elemental existential question and one that begins our effort to understand who we are online. How are our online personas related to our offline selves? Is there one unifying self that is the "true" identity?

Carl Jung (1875–1961) considered that one's *persona* is like a mask that we put on to create a public image of ourselves in a particular context. He said, *"One could say, with a little exaggeration, that the persona is that which in reality one is not, but which oneself as well as others think one is"* (Jung, McGuire, Read, Fordham, & Adler, 1969).

William James (1842–1910) also believed that we have as many "social selves" as we do social situations (Comello, 2009). The idea that we have multiple personas is not new, but how those personas are created and maintained online is the subject of this chapter. Note that I use the terms *persona* and *identity* interchangeably.

When we move to the digital universe, we have both context and audience, and how we construct the identity we present in those situations is our focus here. I propose that not only are there differences in the context and audience by available platforms, but we also carefully choose how we convey our identity in different platforms. For example, Facebook may be the space where I share relatively benign content (photos of family, newsy items, funny videos) while saving more politically oriented posts for Twitter. On some sites, one can choose (by filtering) who can view posts, allowing for different impressions to be created for different subgroups of friends.

Social media is not free of societal ills and in some cases is an amplification of those. While activists and those promoting a cause can gain support (financial, petition signatures, etc.), the systemic ills are not absent from the digital world. Racism, sexism, oppression, and perpetuation of stereotypes occur online as they do offline. Marwick (2013) argues that when the traditional categories of identity (gender, race, sexuality, education) are not apparent, there is a widespread assumption that the person is a straight White male.

We must remember that the online persona is not a separate entity from the offline self, and that the developments and expressions in one context influence the evolving persona in the other domain. Wittkower (2014) believes that the multiple online identities are actually more authentic, disagreeing with Mark Zuckerberg of Facebook who said, "The days of having a different image for your work friends or co-workers and for the other people you know are probably coming to an end pretty quickly. . . . Having two identities for yourself is an example of a lack of integrity" (p. 11).

GOFFMAN'S THEORY

Erving Goffman (1959) examined identity by comparing it to theater productions. In that vein, he proposed that we act differently when on *front stage* before the audience than we do *backstage*. When on front stage, we are aware that we are being observed and act accordingly, generally following the script (social norms and expectations). The goal is to portray the image we want the audience to know (impressions that we deliberately *give*), although we may also create impressions that are unintended (by *giving off* cues that the audience incorporates into their impressions). Backstage, however, we are free of those societal expectations and are no longer "in role." Goffman noted that when we are front stage, we selectively present the more favorable aspects of ourselves, while perhaps de-emphasizing other aspects. This is not being deceptive, he claimed, because both the front and backstage personas are aspects of the same person. Wittkower (2014) weighs in on the front- and back stage distinction, saying that the role we play on front stage is often the persona we aspire to, and thus can be considered the more authentic self. He also believes that there is not a clear demarcation between the two stages, with people moving seamlessly between them.

Although digital technology was not nearly developed in Goffman's time, and computer-mediated communications (CMC) were just becoming widespread, his theory is very relevant to today's digital world and is often cited in the literature. In fact, experts cited by Bullingham and

Vasconcelos (2013) find Goffman's theory to be uniquely applicable to the digital landscape today. They view the backstage locale to be offline, with the front stage to be our online presence. As in offline, Goffman's notion of *face*, the self that one wants to nurture, is like a mask that one puts on for a given performance, and that we do not want to lose (damage the impression we have created.)

CONSTRUCTION OF THE ONLINE PERSONA

Online persona has been described as "the performance of selfhood" (Strangelove, 2010, p. 75), the performance of persona (Marshall, 2014), and the "edited self" (Marwick, 2013). Our online personas are composed of material we select and post (names, photos, links, etc.) and our interactions with others (comments, exchanges), and consistent with Goffman's theory, we vary our persona/identity to suit the context and audience. Marwick (2013) reminds us that early CMC was primarily via text and took place in chat rooms and MUDs (multiuser dungeon games). Some experts believed that the ability to communicate with others whose physical characteristics could reveal much about their identity (race, gender, disability, age group) if they were visible would inhibit discrimination because those characteristics were unknown. Others thought that many people would experiment with identities that varied in significant ways from their offline identity, using the opportunity to experiment with alternative selves.

However, Marwick (2013) notes that most people's online personas in the early days of CMC were quite similar to their offline ones, and discrimination was not noticeably curtailed. She points out that the current versions of social media, such as Facebook, require users to provide real-life details, as do several other sites. Wittkower (2014) observes the changes that were brought about by Facebook and are now common in social media: the use of real names, using photos as avatars, the restricted format of profiles, the presence of tagging, and the need to opt out to limit that practice. While the decision to require actual identification when signing up may have been for marketing purposes that allow advertisers to reach a target group, it also serves the purpose of reducing the proportion of social media participants who can be truly anonymous. Whether people include photos or other data regarding group membership becomes an important individual decision in creating the online persona.

An interesting observation about online presentations of the self is that on popular platforms like Facebook and Twitter, one's "friends" are all in one group (what Wittkower calls "the promiscuous intermixing of audiences" (p. 6), whereas in offline life, many people have multiple groups of friends that share a specific feature (e.g., they love tennis) but that are unknown to other groups of friends (college friends). On these sites, it is uncommon for users to restrict their posts or data to subgroups of friends, which affects their choices (Wittkower, 2014). Rui and Stefanone (2013) refer to this as the *multiple audience problem*: Different groups of friends have different expectations of one's persona. It is also important to realize that one's persona is not only communicated via shared information and user behavior but includes information that others "give off" by tagging them in photos, posting on their walls, and by making comments about their content or posts. Rui and Stefanone propose that the ability of others to contribute to one's pages reduces the degree of control the owner of the page has. They distinguish between self-provided information and other-provided information in discussing this feature. These researchers also suggest that personas can be acquisitive, approval-seeking, or protective, avoiding disapproval. These motives influence the choices for self-presentation and exposure. Another goal is attention seeking, which is associated with those who engage in *promiscuous friending* to gain more attention, and those users are closely checking comments and "likes" in an effort to meet their goal. Such persons tend to post more frequently, especially as they have large audiences and need to maintain the relationships.

Individuals, especially on Facebook, have choices about how to present themselves (Wittkower, 2014). *Mixed exposure* is a strategy in which one posts comments on others without considering how various friends (or friends of friends) might interpret or react to the posting. One can perhaps limit the potential offenses by choosing to friend only those who share important values and perspectives. The strategy of *agonistic exposure* is one where one shares aspects of self that one might not usually share or make public. This can lead to alienation or unfriending from others and damage some relationships. On the other hand, sharing a persona that includes aspects that may be repugnant to some might lead to deeper relationships with others. We will see that this appears to be the approach taken by Trump, whose posts offend many followers but are enthusiastically approved by a core and loyal group. The final strategy is the *lowest common denominator* strategy, in which we present only a bland, acceptable persona to avoid the possibly offending someone. I confess that I used this strategy when I first started using social media, avoiding anything that could be contentious or provocative to anyone. I have long since abandoned that strategy, knowing I have lost some friends—but gained others.

Wittkower (2014) described four strategies of online identity construction. He calls the first *the spectacular identity*, by which he means one that portrays a persona who is special, is talented, and who has admirable experiences and achievements. Wittkower implies that spectacular identities are a "groomed identity manufactured as a consumable product," similar to those of celebrities who present a very carefully packaged online image. The strategy of the *untidy identity* involves frequent posting, sharing, and engaging in other interactions in social media that do not seek the unitary and organized presentation of the spectacular self. This strategy is characterized by tagging and posting by others, and by over-sharing, or revealing aspects of self that might be more appropriate for a smaller group of friends than the entire Facebook audience. Wittkower considers the untidy identity to be proactive, whereas the *distributed identity* is reactive. One with a distributed identity engages in the social network by commenting on other's posts or posting on others' walls rather than posting status updates and other content. This strategy allows the user to protect the persona by carefully picking and choosing how to participate, looking engaged while revealing little. Finally, there is the *minimized identity*. This is used by one who participates only peripherally, posts very little (may not even have a profile picture), but peruses the posts of others. This person looks to social networks for information but not interaction. Some would call this lurking.

Moore, Barbour, and Lee (2017) propose that there are five dimensions of online persona. The first dimension is *publicness,* which is the nature of most social media today. More and more sites require real data about users and have statements about the public nature of the site in their user agreements (usually unread). In addition, tracking practices on numerous digital devices collect information about users. People who use multiple social media and also enjoy such technological innovations as smart watches, Fitbits, GPS, and use search engines are contributing to what Moore et al. refer to as "networked selves." At the center of these networks are the *micropublics* or the connections among personal friends, professional colleagues, and others with whom one interacts. The degree of publicness ranges from a small group to a global audience, and knowledge of this impacts the nature of material one shares.

The next dimension is the *mediatized* dimension. Moore et al. (2017) point out that people are now quite skilled at the various ways in which one can use social media to share their self-image widely. Many hope that exposure to large audiences will lead to fame and fortune, which has occurred with some individuals who use YouTube to generate a fan base or enjoy generating conflict and controversy on Twitter. The ability to "sell" oneself to the public was once the exclusive feat of known celebrities from other media (film, television, politics) but such restrictions no longer exist.

The *performative* dimension closely parallels Goffman's theory, described earlier. It refers to the front- and backstage distinction, and the importance of roles and face. These authors noted that when our public roles are enacted online and interact with others' public personas, a pattern of communication that may become the norm for that relationship. They also note that every aspect of text contributes to the persona, from the word choices, use of emojis or gifs or capital letters, tone of comments, and so on. Goffman's notion of performing means that the many voices and ways of expressing oneself online must be frequently moderated to ensure that the persona is "sincere and authentic" (p. 5).

The *collective* dimension is the dimension that engages in different social networks that overlap but is anchored in the user's persona. Within this dimension user's micropublics are connected via images, likes, selfies, and so forth. Micropublics are network affiliations that are updated and current, and reflect awareness of the different audiences in each. Twitter is widely used by journalists, professionals often use LinkedIn, and professors use academia.edu. The public persona is an outgrowth or collective of the different networks.

The final dimension of Moore et al.'s (2017) model, the *value* dimension, assumes that the persona is created for a specific intent (e.g., personal, professional, celebrity). The user produces a persona by actively deciding what actions to take (posting a status update, sharing a post, liking others' statuses, commenting, sharing photos) that creates the persona, to which is attached a reputation and prestige. The value of a persona is determined by the extent to which it achieved the original intent for creating it.

AVATARS

One online element that brings the idea of persona to life is that of the *avatar*. While avatars are created for specific contexts, the decisions the user makes about the appearance and behavior of the avatar are instructive for understanding the concept of online persona. Although avatars do not necessarily contain characteristics of their creators, the choices of avatar appearance and behavior reveal much about the person behind the creation (Smith & Watson, 2014).

While anyone can create an avatar and use it for a profile picture, for example, in virtual worlds they are a necessity. There are several types of virtual words: those in massively multiplayer online role-playing games (MMORPGs) like *World of Warcraft* and creativity-oriented environments such as *Second Life* for adults and *Whyville* for young people (Lin & Wang, 2014). These researchers define an avatar (which has its etymological origins in Hindu) as "any form of representation that marks a user's identity" (p. 213), that more commonly refers to the digital depiction of people in virtual worlds. The possibilities for avatars have evolved from two-dimensional symbols to elaborate and customizable 3-D figures, and users can experiment and create their avatars to present a persona with a specific look, personality, and behaviors that will interact with others in their chosen environment. Players or inhabitants of virtual worlds create this representation of themselves by considering the situation and portraying characteristics that are suited for that setting.

Lin and Wang (2014) refer to previous research that described three factors that influence the avatar's creation: some users create an avatar that presents their *ideal self*, possessing the qualities that creator wishes to have; other users wish to stand out in some way, or to be noticed and considered unique; and the third motivation is to model one's avatar/persona against that of a real or virtual celebrity or to fit in with a trend. Another study looked at teen's reasons for the design of their avatars for Whyville. net. Some inhabitants were interested in the artistic or design features, without concern for resemblance to the offline self, while others did include aspects of their "real" self. Some chose their avatar's features to show allegiance to a person or a group, while others included features they cannot obtain offline, and still others chose to join with or oppose what they see as a current trend in the world. Finally, there are those who deliberately disguise their identity.

Lin and Wang (2014) recruited 244 users of virtual worlds for their survey. They discovered that about 64% of participants described their avatar as a human being, while 34% indicated their avatar was an animal and 2% reported their avatar was not a living being. Most respondents (58%) had one or two avatars, while 12% had more than five. The avatars chosen by participants were generally quite different from their offline appearance, and moderately similar in personality. The factor analysis of their survey of motivations for avatar creation resulted in four factors: virtual exploration, social navigation, contextual adaptation, and identity representation. The first included the desire to present themselves as unconventional or unique, and to explore roles they are unable to enact offline. Social navigation refers to the presentation of someone who wishes to make friends and construct a reputation in the virtual world. The contextual adaptation refers to the wish to present a persona that is consistent with the social environment of the platform. The final factor focused on how the individual decided whether to present their actual self, their idealized self, or emphasize a particular characteristic. This suggests that avatars in virtual worlds are one type of persona found online. These are consciously created to describe a particular persona and provide insight into the cognitive processes that determine what the avatar becomes.

SOCIAL MEDIA

Social media platforms provide another perspective on how online personas are derived. For example, Facebook provides several ways for users to present themselves: their profile provides information, as do their photos and video posts, status updates, comments, shared memes and news items, and others. In addition, such data as the number of "friends" one has conveys information; having very few friends and a very large number of friends might be negatively evaluated by users of the site, the former suggesting isolation and the latter pointing to superficial connections made just to look well known. The persona may be one that exaggerates positive qualities, or one that portrays an honest image.

Kim and Lee (2011) examined self-presentation on Facebook in a sample of 391 college students. Their analysis showed that the number of Facebook friends was positively associated with subjective well-being. The more Facebook friends, the happier the user. They also discovered that the number of friends also was related to the belief that those friends provide social support, but that relation did not hold when the number of friends became too high. The researchers speculate that when one has a great many friends, one cannot devote enough time to maintaining each relationship. Finally, the type of self-presentation had differential associations with subjective well-being, so that positive self-presentation directly predicted subjective well-being, but honest self-presentation influenced well-being through perceived social support. It may be that honest self-presentation includes disclosing troubles or stressors, which leads friends to respond with supportive comments or other gestures.

The presentation of the online self requires adjustments to each unique platform, as different media have different affordances (possible actions allowed by the infrastructure) and different expectations for behavior. People typically present a very professional persona on a site such as LinkedIn, while Facebook personas are often more social. Even communications on professional topics have a different tone on Facebook than on LinkedIn. Facebook "friends" are predominantly offline friends as well (Marwick, 2013), so often statuses include material about family, vacations, activities, and other mundane details.

Celebrities

What qualifies someone to be called a celebrity? Marwick and Boyd (2011) propose that there are three defining characteristics: the way someone is discussed and considered, the commodification of the persona, and a feature of our culture, in which certain people are elevated and acquire a legion of fans.

As of February 2019, all but one (Barack Obama) of the ten Twitter accounts with the most followers are those of entertainment celebrities, with Katy Perry and Justin Bieber in the first and second places, respectively (Statista.com, 2019). Social media are an important means for celebrities to create and maintain their public persona. Moore et al. (2017) point out that this is not a task typically managed by the celebrity, but by teams of staff dedicated to this job. The public personas of celebrities are formed of a collection of *paratexts*, which are elements that are used to promote themselves and their uniqueness. They are revealed in posts, images, and in promotion of offline media events such as television broadcasts of award ceremonies at which the celebrity was honored, had a role, wore a spectacular outfit. When these promotions are then re-broadcast on online video channels, they are often edited to present the most effective view.

The use of social media by celebrities is described by Marwick and Boyd (2011) as a practice rather than a status. That is, celebrities actively perform their personas to ensure the continuance and expansion of their fan bases and to give access to the persona they construct for that purpose. The use of Twitter allows celebrities to create the illusion of giving access to their backstage (as per Goffman) lives so the fans feel a personal connection to their celebrities. What is actually front stage or backstage is not always clear, as it varies by "audience, context, and interpretation" (Marwick & Boyd, 2011, p. 144).

Celebrities are vulnerable to having fake accounts created in their names, and although most celebrities maintain their own Twitter accounts, some have employees to do so. In some cases, they are simply too busy to participate but know how useful the engagement with an audience can be, while others have contracts that prohibit tweeting, and some have managers who discourage the practice. The practice of maintaining the persona involves replies to other tweets (a coup for a fan is to receive a reply from a celebrity or to be mentioned by one), or to retweet and use hashtags. The role of the celebrity is to create a persona for fans that appears sincere and authentic. Sometimes spats with other celebrities will be performed on Twitter, providing gossip and a sense of insider status to fans. Celebrities will sometimes post images to give followers a sense of intimate knowledge, although those are generally carefully curated and selected for that purpose.

Microcelebrities

Becoming famous online is possible when someone attracts a great deal of attention to their online persona. A striking example of this phenomenon is that of the *hijabistas* (Kavakci & Kraeplin, 2017). The term is a blend of the *hijab* (headscarf worn by some Muslim women) and *fashionista* (a woman who knows and sports current and cutting-edge fashion); it refers to Muslim women who adhere to religious notions of modesty while also being very stylish. Sometimes their images include activities not typically thought of in association with Muslim women (e.g., skateboarding). Their virtual personas are intended to debunk Western stereotypes and to add their voice to the socialization of young Muslim women that is influenced by digital media. These women must negotiate a careful balance between their mediatized Western identity and their religious Muslim identity. Nevertheless, they follow the pattern of other digital microcelebrities: Construct a careful profile, reach out to potential followers, share personal information to create a relationship with followers, and so on. Several of the hijabistas have very large followings, and one even has more than a million. They use Twitter and Instagram, but also Facebook and YouTube to share their personas. At one point, a video of the hijabistas was posted online and generated considerable controversy. There were some who found their attire and behavior immodest and inappropriate for religious Muslim women and others who supported their portrayal of a more modern persona.

There is another category of celebrities, those who use YouTube to amass a large following in the hopes of becoming an *influencer*—a person who is paid to display brands in their videos due to their large following. Smith (2014) refers to this practice as "self-commodification," that is accomplished by the creation of a persona that is a kind of brand. Smith presents a case study of a particularly successful YouTuber, who was granted "partner status" by YouTube and was paid to post his vlogs (video logs). García-Rapp and Roca-Cuberes (2017) published an ethnographic study of a highly successful beauty guru on YouTube: Bubz. Bubz is a British-Chinese purveyor of beauty tips about makeup, hairstyles, and cosmetics. Her YouTube channels have over 2.5 million subscribers and have been viewed more than 400 million times. As is true of other microcelebrities, she must balance the persona of an ordinary person with that of an expert, and must constantly work to maintain that persona by sharing details of her daily life so that viewers feel as though they "know her."

These researchers examined Bubz's video contents and categorized them as motivational, relational, content-oriented, and market-oriented. The role of a microcelebrity requires daily attention, which Goffman would call daily performance. She also needs comments, which are also a way to demonstrate her popularity and the huge number of followers but cannot respond to each individually. She demonstrates her commitment to her audience by making appreciative reference to her loyal audience, and posting some Q&A videos to let the audience know she is responsive to them.

Politicians' Personas

If ordinary people spend time and energy creating and maintaining an online persona, consider what is needed by an entertainer or politician whose reputation makes their persona an important vehicle for self-promotion. This is clearly important to Trump, who conducts business and foreign policy on Twitter, making his followers feel as though they are insiders. The political use of social media extends far beyond buying advertising on social media or posting campaign speeches on YouTube but focuses on direct communication with the target audience without censorship or editorial corrections.

This is clearly important to Trump, who conducts business and foreign policy on Twitter, making his followers feel as though they are insiders.

Donald Trump is not the first politician to use social media to express a persona. Dow (2017) argues that it was the persona, more than the content of the media, that was influential in the 2016 election campaign. She says, "What if they were voting for a person, not a set of policies?" (p. 137). Trump's persona was that of an outsider to politics, a businessman and reality TV celebrity, one who makes deals and gets things done by the force of his personality. Dow believes that voters who were frustrated with politics were enamored of this persona, which was in stark contrast to Hillary Clinton's persona as a policy wonk and "incumbent." Trump's continued and incessant use of Twitter to reinforce that persona is evident in his May 2018 status as the world leader with the most followers (his personal account has 52 million) on Twitter, followed by Pope Francis, Narendra Modi of India, and the official presidential account (Statista.com, 2019).

Hong and Nadler (2011) observe that Barack Obama had more than 100 people dedicated to working on social media during his presidential campaign, and that Nancy Pelosi announced her decision to run for House Minority Leader on Twitter. Twitter differs from Facebook and some other sites in that a tweet can be seen by anyone (not just "friends" or those with permission) that makes it particularly appealing to politicians. Prior research about the use of Twitter by political figures found that almost half of politicians' tweets were links to other sites or information about media appearances (television or radio interviews). Only 1.4% of tweets from members of Congress were responses to tweets they received.

Hong and Nadler (2011) attempted to assess the influence of tweets of nine Republican politicians for whom there were consistent opinion polls in the period of interest (2009–2011). They used the number of tweets posted during the time period for which the opinion polls were available. They controlled for other media coverage aside from social media. Their results showed that there was no evidence that the number of tweets was associated with a change in public opinion.

Marshall and Henderson (2016) offer a perspective on the personas of Trump and Hillary Clinton, and how social media were the platform on which the personas were promoted. Marshall and Henderson (2016), and Smith (2017), opine that the way these two politicians used social media during the campaign for the 2016 election was very similar to the way celebrities operate online. The operational definition of persona in these papers is "a strategic identity, a form of negotiation of the individual in their foray into a collective world of the social." From that perspective, the persona is very much a mask, worn for the wooing of the audience. Interestingly, more traditional media (newspapers and television) now look to social media for breaking news, knowing that events will appear online instantaneously, and they need to pay attention to be relevant.

Trump brought his persona of the entertainment celebrity to the political arena, widening the audience to include the electorate. He brought his tools for attracting attention, expressing emotions, and building an audience of followers. Marshall and Henderson (2016) refer to this process of using technology to expand the audience *mediatization*. They also believe that the political persona is not only a feature of politicians, but of all social media users, since they engage with the politicians and each other about candidates and issues on multiple platforms.

Trump was a media personality with a public persona long before social media existed. He was often on national television, selling the persona of "successful businessman." He bought the Miss American beauty pageant, which was covered by the traditional media. His most recent media persona was as "the boss," on the reality show *The Apprentice*, where he was decisive and fearless, expanding his "businessman" persona. Marshall and Henderson (2016) note that Trump's use of the traditional media made him a celebrity, which transferred easily to the online context, where he added his contempt for the established norms and practices of political power. His disdain for tradition and etiquette and his many unilateral decisions upending established policy and international relationships drew constant attention. His tweets were often outrageous, which attracted the attention of traditional media, expanding his audience. Trump appeared to deliberately create chaos and instability, while Clinton's persona was of a seasoned and reasonable politician. Apparently, Trump's persona was attractive and compelling for the angry and disillusioned voters who resonated to his rejection of government-as-usual, since in their view, government as usual had abandoned them (Marshall & Henderson, 2016).

Hillary Clinton's persona was a contrast to that of her opponent. Her persona was that of a seasoned politician, who had served the country in multiple roles, and had experience in all aspects of government. Smith (2017) suggests that Clinton's followers were often young girls—known as fangirls—rather than supporters. She also had celebrity before the campaign, but calling her followers "fangirls" diminished her status. She was savvy in her use of social media, but her persona, as a feminist, experienced political insider whose followers were silly girls who swoon over celebrities in general, worked against her.

ONLINE DATING

Online dating was first thought of as a strategy only for the desperate. Today it is quite commonplace, and many marriages have resulted from couples who initially met online. Nevertheless, the online context presents a unique context for expressing one's persona. Those who visit online dating sites will quickly peruse profiles to select potential partners, so the construction of a profile is a critical task. The challenge is to present one's persona in a positive light while also being honest, because the hope is to meet someone in person at some point, and most people would not respond favorably to having been deceived by an exaggerated or inaccurate profile (Ellison, Hancock, & Toma, 2011). Whitty (2008) also reported that her participants admitted to embellishing or exaggerating in their profile, with about half saying they had misrepresented themselves on the dating site. Some were concerned about the persona they created and asked others to review their profiles to ensure reasonable accuracy.

The question of how much embellishment or deception is acceptable is addressed in a qualitative study of 37 users of online dating sites who were an average of 30 years old with two years of experience on online data sites (Ellison et al., 2011). Participants rated the accuracy of the information in their profile, and then participated in a semi-structured interview with the researchers. Briefly, the daters were asked to comment on those facts that they rated as less accurate. There were several interesting findings. First, participants did not expect the profiles to be a duplication of the offline persona. They recognized that the profile invoked not just the current self, but past and future ones as well. They were forgiving of discrepancies that are malleable (e.g., hairstyle) but less so for unchangeable characteristics (age or height). They were tolerant—and expected—small departures from those figures but took magnitude of the differences into account when deciding whether they were acceptable within the parameters of the dating site. They also recognized that people used word choices to soften a questionable imperfection (e.g., saying "curvy" rather than "overweight"). Taking all their data into account, the researchers concluded that the profile is best viewed as a *promise*, saying:

> The profile constitutes a promise made to an imagined audience that future face-to-face interaction will take place with someone who does not differ fundamentally from the person represented in the profile. (p. 56)

The choice of what to include in the profile is influenced by the degree of self-awareness of the person, the occasional intent to disguise one's identity, and the constraints of the social media platform. However, the fact that one can take the necessary time to construct, revise, select, and reflect upon what to include allows a more thoughtful, rather than spontaneous, profile. One also needs to be mindful of the norms and conventions of the platform, so that the type of audience and the kinds of profiles available impact the decision of a new member of the group.

Toma and Hancock (2010) studied the construction of online dating profiles, with an emphasis on physical attractiveness. The authors note the evolutionary foundation of physical attractiveness as an important marker of a potential mate (signaling health, reproductive capacity, fitness, etc.) and posited that attractiveness is more important for the female in the search for a mate. Sixty participants in an Australian dating site interviewed for a study by Whitty (2008) revealed the paramount importance of physical attractiveness, which was also reflected in their choice of photos to include in the profile. Some (mostly women) participants had professional glamour shots made for this purpose.

The endeavor of looking for a partner online implies that the participant would be motivated to present a positive persona, although users interested in finding a long-term or life partner would be less likely to be deceptive in their profiles because the discovery of the deception in the desired offline meeting could be an impediment to forming a relationship.

Toma and Hancock (2010) studied self-presentation in general online dating platforms (not those for specific subgroups) and noted that one's persona is revealed on such sites in two ways: photographs and verbal descriptions. They note that the online context has several features not present in in-person meetings: Appearance can be enhanced, and the descriptions can be carefully tailored to present the most positive impression. They say that the options to edit before posting and that the posting and viewing are not synchronous are unique to the online dating scene.

In their study of 80 users of online dating sites, using clever and appropriate methodology, the researchers found that as predicted, subjects who were less physically attractive engaged in more enhancement of their photos and descriptions, and that women did so more often than men. However, those who were interested in finding a long-term relationship engaged in less enhancement. Furthermore, participants who were more attractive, and those seeking long-term relationships, posted more photos. However, contrary to their prediction that less attractive participants would compensate in their presentation of social status as indicated by occupation, income, and education, this hypothesis was not substantiated.

SUMMARY

Everyone with a presence on social media has constructed a persona, and the performance of that persona is ongoing, with most users working to present a coherent identity. We know that the persona includes not just what a user chooses to include, but what actions he or she engages in, and the comments and interactions with others. Different online platforms call for somewhat different personas, and we are all sensitive to those expectations. However, offline celebrities maintain a presence online, and online celebrities (microcelebrities) work to maintain the persona and continue to attract and keep followers. Politicians have in recent years used social media to present their persona directly to their audience, without mediation by editors or other censors. We see that Donald Trump's persona as a brash outsider with an aversion to traditional identities of politicians appears to be rewarded with both a large following and election to the highest office in the country. We contrasted this with the persona of his 2016 presidential opponent, Hillary Clinton, whose persona as an experienced, knowledgeable insider appeared to work against her. Finally, we noted the proliferation of online dating sites, in which the persona either leads to the goal of meeting offline partners or not, and the construction of such identity profiles is a difficult balance between putting forward one's positive features without diverging too much from the offline person. Outright deception on these sites is likely to end in rejection, which is not why people join such sites. Perhaps going forward, readers will pay closer attention to their online personas and check that they are consistent with the impression they want their audience to have.

STORIES OF TWO ACTIVISTS

If you say things of consequence, there may be consequences. The alternative is to be inconsequential.

Katie Orenstein, the OpEd Project

The two profiles in this story are activists for whom the preceding quote is quite salient. When they share content online, they expect there will be opposition to their views, and generally are able to shield themselves with the knowledge that the hatred is not really personal. Nevertheless, their stories are instructive for taking controversial positions online, and for managing digital aggression.

MICHELLE PITOT

Michelle Pitot is a consultant and coach and an adjunct professor in the school of government and public policy at a large university. She also facilitates workshops on topics related to diversity and social justice and is steeped in concerns about systemic oppression in this country. When she was a fellow of the OpEd project she wrote a piece on White fragility that was published in the *Hill*. White fragility refers to the defensive and at times dismissive reaction from White people when they hear about implicit racism, microaggressions, and other ways in which racist attitudes and beliefs—conscious or not, intentional or not—are expressed in our actions.

The article is clearly labeled as an opinion piece, and Pitot knew that there would be readers who would disagree with her perspective. What she did not anticipate was the quantity of comments (there were 600+) and the ways in which the online dialog veered away from her points. At first, she was offended, but quickly recognized that the comments were not about her, and not even about her article. They were the kinds of angry comments that appear online that express the underlying angers and frustrations of people who perhaps do not have outlets elsewhere for those feelings.

Pitot was advised not to read the comments, as others know that there are likely to be critical or worse remarks that can be upsetting. She ignored that advice because she felt she could learn something from them, particularly given her work to help people confront these difficult concepts. There were a few of the comments that tried to rebut the critics, and Pitot hopes that a reader who might not post a comment themselves but would read them would recognize something of value in those comments.

Despite the onslaught of negative reactions, Pitot is glad that her OpEd attracted so many readers and hopes that some were able to increase their awareness of an issue that seems to be particularly important in today's political climate.

NOLAN CABRERA

Nolan Cabrera is a tenured faculty member at a large university who has always been outspoken about the concerns of marginalized communities, and about Whiteness in higher education. His recent book, *White Guys on Campus*, has increased the size of his audience and has perhaps increased attention to his online presence. He posts on Facebook, Twitter, Instagram, and YouTube. However, it was a very brief appearance on Fox News that garnered the most reaction.

The clip was viewed in real time by some, but as with anything available online, it can be linked in messages or posts and shared widely. In the interview clip, Cabrera commented on a policy at the University of Chicago regarding trigger warnings and safe spaces on campus. The policy recognizes that some content may elicit strong emotional reactions among students, and requires instructors to give advance notice if such content is included in a course. The underlying belief is that classrooms and campuses should be safe spaces where students' emotional equilibrium is not at risk. Cabrera simply said in the interview that there was a reason safe spaces were needed. Most of the responses came to him via his university voicemail (which is public information) and included accusations that he was an affront to God because he supported LGBT+ persons, with many references to the Bible, ad hominem attacks ("You seem like a smart guy. Maybe your ponytail is pulled too tight), and veiled threats such as "You'll be hearing more from me my friend, you better believe that."

In another interview, this time in the *Chronicle of Higher Education*, Cabrera talked about the practice of "progressive stacking." That means that the amount of air time a student usually gets in class is the privilege of some social identities, so that the voices of students with marginalized identities are often not heard. Progressive stacking means acknowledging this in class and making a practice of inviting more participation from those students who ordinarily would be overlooked. Cabrera's comments were included in a column by a well-known conservative columnist, Ben Shapiro, which again widened the audience and increased the volume of voicemail. Many of the messages were incoherent, but angry.

Despite the abundance of negative and aggressive responses he receives, Cabrera has not thought of censoring himself or silencing his voice. He believes that even among the derogatory comments, a silent reader may find something of value. He typically doesn't respond to tweets or comments that attack him, and finds Twitter to be a useful platform to get his message out. Some of the comments are genuine requests for clarification, and he doesn't want to miss an opportunity to educate an interested reader. The trick is to be able to distinguish a genuine request for information from the troll who is seeking to hook him into a meaningless and distracting exchange. He says, "I do have a responsibility to the interest of the public discourse" so he will continue to navigate that fine line.

Among other digital platforms Cabrera has used, his TED talk, "White Immunity Working through the Pitfalls of 'Privilege Discourse,'" was posted on YouTube, and of course elicited the usual type of comments:

This guy's "intellectual journey" went about five feet and then crapped its diapers.
    Nolan Cuckles. Fairy pants la la la.
    remember kids, only white people are capable of wrong doing.

However, there were also a few positive remarks:

Enjoyed listening to your talk on White Immunity.
    He is speaking a lot of truth although he does come across as playing a blame game at first but if you hear him through. He is speaking in honest laymen terms that a lot of privileged people don't want to hear.
    If privilege is normal in your life, equity feels like oppression—the internet philosopher anonymous.

I have several thoughts about those who post these comments. First, the title of the TED talk identifies the subject of the talk quite clearly. It is obvious that some of the distractors view the talk with the intention of being critical, as their disagreement (rather than curiosity) drives their interest in the talk. Second, the nature of the comments suggests that for some, the chance to be glib or amusing is part of the appeal. Perhaps this is a case where the asynchronous nature of the exchange allows the commenter to take time to compose what they think is a clever riposte. In person, that same individual may not be able to compose such a response in the moment.

Cabrera's commitment and determination to disseminate his message is admirable, particularly knowing that aggressive responses are almost guaranteed. The quote at the beginning of this story is especially apt in Cabrera's case.

6

Trolling

Trolling, an internet slang term that has been used since the early 1990s, is a form of cyberaggression that is related to, but different from, cyberbullying. Ekstrand (2018) dates the first use of the term to 1992 on a message board when a user posted, "Maybe after I post it, we could go trolling some more and see what happens" (p. 52). Zezulka and Seigfried-Spellar (2016) distinguish trolls from cyberbullies by whether the target is known to the perpetrator offline. They posit that when the target is known to the perpetrator, the behavior should be considered cyberbullying, but when the target or targets are unknown, trolling is the appropriate term. Cyberbullies have a more personal agenda of hostility toward the target, while trolls' attacks may appear random and pointless (Jussinoja, 2018). The power differential between perpetrator and target that is a characteristic of cyberbullying is not relevant in the troll dynamic.

Phillips (2011) points out that the distinction between trolls and cyberbullies is of more than semantic interest. Trolling in the United States is generally protected by free speech, she says, whereas cyberbullying is more likely to be illegal (e.g., online harassment is illegal, as is inciting violence). I disagree with both of those positions. First, trolls often attack specific individuals whom they deem deserving of their rebuke, and sometimes "gang up" to engage in troll wars on individuals. Second, trolling can also be harassment and can incite violence. In fact, an internet troll in the United Kingdom was convicted of trolling and jailed for 18 weeks. I propose that the distinction between cyberbullying and trolling lies in the goal—trolls aim to provoke, to disrupt, to cause others to react, all in the service of attention and the delight in others' humiliation. The cyberbully intends to harm a specific individual.

DEFINITIONS

Because trolling, which has been practiced now for many years, has evolved in response to increased affordances that have emerged as social media have developed and changed, scholars suggest that a consensus on a definition is impossible. That is, what is considered trolling depends on the time, the platform, the community, and even the personality of the poster. What follows in this chapter should be read with that caveat in mind.

Trolling refers to online behaviors that are intentionally disruptive and that attempt to lure unsuspecting participants into being exposed as naïve and gullible. Merrin (2019) defines it this way: "Trolling, therefore, is a baiting, a sport, a playing, that more than anything aims at those who get above themselves, or set themselves above others—at those asserting, or in, authority" (p. 202). People who routinely engage in this behavior, and who often self-identify with this practice, are known as trolls (Phillips, 2011). Among other things, trolls resent any kind of regulations and rules, and rebel against "political correctness" and oversight or moderation of cyberspace. Trolls are usually anonymous; anonymity is important to trolls because they rely on duping their prey to demonstrate their own wit and cleverness—and if their identity were known, they could not pretend to be sincerely interested to fool those they are targeting (a key component of the troll's toolkit). Trolls operate by engaging in arguments (although they do not care about the topic), leading the discussion in an unproductive direction, and sometimes engaging in personal attacks to provoke a reaction (outrage, often) in other participants. That is the mark of a successful troll—tricking other participants into reacting to their bogus posts.

Trolls enjoy the attention they get from their obnoxious behavior and so often choose topics or discussions of topics of high current media interest because they anticipate that their behavior will be reported by traditional media, sending more viewers to their "work." They also sometimes target well-known persons or celebrities, because they have very large numbers of followers, some of whom will engage in the sought-after argument or will spread the content to even more viewers (Kopecký, 2016).

Several researchers believe that the definition of trolls and trolling should be based on what those participating in online trolling activities have to say. To that end Hardaker (2010) collected public use data from a Usenet group and searched for the words *troll* and derivatives (over 2,000 found among 186,470 posts covering nine years). Hardaker found four themes in those posts: deception, aggression, disruption, and success.

Deception is evident in their posing as sincere participants (and often also in taking false identities). Aggression is seen in the nasty and vulgar language, and in the ad hominem attacks on other posters to a discussion. Disruption is commonly used to derail a discussion by introducing extraneous topics, bringing up irrelevant information, and refusing to respond directly when queried. Success is the ultimate satisfaction the troll experiences when their deception, aggression, and disruption provoke emotional responses from others, and when their trolling products receive wide attention.

In focus groups and interviews with college students, Sanfilippo, Fichman, and Yang (2018) reported that their subjects agreed that the essential nature of trolling is provocative, enacted by taking the opposing opinion to generate reactions. Interestingly, the participants in their qualitative study reported that there are two types of trolls: the malevolent troll (the typical stereotypical trolls who "mock and degrade") and the "lighthearted" troll (p. 31), who is playful and finds humor (often satire) and entertainment in the disruption. The participants in this study were very clear that people can occasionally engage in trolling without being a troll. That is, the behaviors, when done occasionally, do not merit the label, as that requires persistent and usually mean-spirited activity online. In their conclusion, these researchers determine the element of pseudo-sincerity to be the defining characteristic of trolling.

The Term *Troll*

The origin of the term *troll* is instructive. The *troll* is a creature from Norse (Scandinavian) mythology who has a human-like appearance. Two kinds of trolls have been described. One is huge, ugly, not very intelligent, and usually found hiding under bridges, while cave trolls are rather small (think dwarf), antisocial, argumentative, and, like their larger version, also not very bright. Trolls of both types are demonic at worst and mischievous at best and have a reputation for tormenting travelers. The application to the digital environment is straightforward. Trolls are mischievous characters (or evil, depending on their behavior) who disrupt the online experience of visitors to the World Wide Web.

A likely origin of the verb form, *trolling*, is a method of fishing in

> The *troll* is a creature from Norse (Scandinavian) mythology who has a human-like appearance. Two kinds of trolls have been described. One is huge, ugly, not very intelligent, and usually found hiding under bridges, while cave trolls are rather small (think dwarf), antisocial, argumentative, and, like their larger version, also not very bright.

which a boat moves through the water slowly, dragging a fishing lure or baited hook. Unwary fish get caught. Again, this applies very well to the trolling seen online. The troll dangles the bait (a seemingly innocent comment) and when the fish (participant in online forum) bites (reacts), the naïve user has been caught and the troll is victorious. Trolls often try to engage with "newbies," new users of a given platform that may not recognize the cues that more experienced users notice to identify a comment as trolling, or the source as a troll. Thus, new users are often embarrassed, some to the point of leaving the group. To execute their attacks, trolls are typically anonymous.

Trolling first emerged in Usenet, which was an early social network for hosting discussions on a variety of topics (and was also a file sharing space). It is an interesting side note that Usenet was developed by university graduate students to facilitate sharing of files and messages with colleagues. Like Facebook several decades later, it spread far beyond the initial college campus community. Early trolls were called Meowers, who disrupted discussion boards with extraneous text, quotes from Monty Python, insults, and nonsense about a cat named Fluffy (hence the name).

Changing Use of the Term

At first, trolls were people who delighted in disrupting discussions, posting outrageous comments that provoked other users, and initiating arguments that could devolve into personal attacks. The topic of the argument was incidental; what mattered was the upheaval the troll generated. Brown (2017) likened trolling to prank phone calls. If the recipient "got the joke" the troll was disappointed, but if they took the bait and reacted, the troll was a success. Early trolls were often humorous, but the emphasis has shifted to the nastier activities. It has been said that trolls do it "for the lulz," which is their term for LOLs (which is too mundane and trite for their taste). That is, they get their enjoyment from abusing others and observing their reactions.

There are sites that are inhabited by trolls, who share successes and support one another's activities. These individuals self-identify as trolls, which is a source of pride. According to Phillips (2011), they are "intelligent, are playful and mischievous and wildly antagonistic" (p. 69). 4chan/b/ is one of the best-known communities of trolls.

Over time, though, the term began to be applied in a more general sense to describe a person who loves provoking reactions (usually angry ones) in others; when people reacted, the troll finds evidence of his or her superiority (they were cleverer than the people who fell for the lure). Brown (2017, paragraph 27) puts it succinctly: "When I see the word troll in a headline, I don't think of a mischievous prankster. The word troll makes me think of vicious sexism, racism, violence, and hate." However, Bishop (2014) defined the term as it is currently used as "the posting of any content on the Internet that is either provocative or offensive" (p. 2).

Trolls also constitute a "subculture" online whose goal is to obtain *lulz*, laughs at someone else's expense (Phillips, 2011). Bishop (2014) has created a typology of trolls, some of whom have positive roles. Readers interested in the nuances of trolling are directed to Bishop's chapter. He refers to Trolls (capital *T*) as the more "classical" type, and trolls (little *t*) as those who occasionally indulge in posting offensive content. Trolls endeavor to disrupt an online community but may explain that their goal is actually "exposing hypocrisy" (Begley, 2017). It is interesting to note that not all scholars (and digitally engaged users) would agree that trolling is always negative. In the Sanfilippo et al. (2018) study, one of their most salient findings is that participants disagreed with prevailing negative perceptions of trolls. They argued that the most extreme examples of trolling (e.g., RIP trolls, discussed later) have tainted the reputation of trolls and lamented that trolling is misunderstood by older generations. The participants acknowledged that trolls go after inexperienced members of a group (and tend to target females more than males), while cyberbullies have a personal reason for selecting their targets, and felt that while occasional trolling, especially within a group of friends, was appropriate, the lone troll was not approved of.

TYPES OF TROLLS

Karppi (2013) described two types of trolls who use Facebook as a platform. These are the RIP trolls and the doppelgänger troll. The first is malicious, and the second is more playful and just annoying. RIP trolls break all the norms around appropriate behaviors when someone dies. Doppelganger trolls harass their namesake with repeated friend requests.

RIP Trolls

RIP trolls target profiles or websites devoted to mourning deceased persons. Most often, these are cases of deaths that have garnered wide media coverage, so the troll anticipates a large vulnerable audience. Phillips (2011) explains the way this practice, and the opportunity to engage in it, emerged on Facebook, which is where much of this activity takes place. Prior to October 2009, Facebook did not do anything about the death of a subscriber. That meant that other subscribers would sometimes get reminders to reconnect with that individual due to algorithms that noted when a subscriber had not been in touch. When some Facebook members got such reminders to reconnect with Facebook friends who were dead, they complained—and Facebook responded. Facebook then allowed friends and families to "memorialize" the deceased's account; no reminders would be sent, only preexisting Facebook friends could visit the wall, no new potential friends could find the profile, and no one could log on to the deceased's page to post.

While this was a step forward, Facebook made an additional modification; friends or family could create an RIP page, which allowed anyone to post thoughts and condolences in one collection. Thus was borne the RIP page, which, in addition to providing a mourning space for those grieving the loss, created an opportunity for trolls to disrupt a sincere and emotional event. Phillips (2011) noted that the traditional media coverage of the death of Dawn Brancheau in 2010 by a killer whale at a SeaWorld show produced a series of offensive posts using Photoshopped images and videos as well as text and memes. No long after, RIP pages were created around a teenager's disappearance (Chelsea King), and things got even uglier when her body was found a week later.

Trolls do what most would think of as unspeakable things on these pages. They may deface photos of the deceased, post photos of grisly accident scenes on the page of someone who was killed in an accident, insert clips from videos that show suicides, post parodies of the way in which someone died (fish with someone's face Photoshopped for someone who drowned), create cruel memes, and other malicious actions. They have promoted conspiracy theories on the sites of children killed at Sandy Hook and Stoneman Douglas schools, saying that the events did not occur and so on. RIP trolls have indicated that their purpose is not to hurt the truly bereaved, but to mock the "grief tourists," who visit and post on RIP sites even though they did not know the individual at all. Some trolls have created RIP pages for persons they made up, with the goal of bringing grief tourists to the site to be attacked.

One example of this kind of trolling occurred following the death of Robin Williams, the well-known actor and comedian. His daughter Zelda Williams posted a tribute to her father on social media. Among the supportive messages she received were the nasty remarks of trolls that were so upsetting she was "left shaking" and deleted her social media accounts to protect herself from further assaults. Some of the messages placed blame on Zelda for her father's death, and others included edited photos of what was supposed to be his dead body with bruises on his neck as if from hanging. Another example is that of Matthew Kocher, a 15-year-old high school student who drowned in Lake Michigan while at a camp. A memorial page dedicated to him included such posts as a meme showing a submerged person's hand breaking through the water with text reading "LOL u drowned you fail at being a fish" (Pratt, 2013). An epilogue to these incidents and others is that when reported to Facebook, the offensive pages are removed (although perhaps not as quickly as family would hope), and families may create new, closed groups for which they control access. The Kochers said that some members of the new group contributed photos they had never seen and stories about their son, which were very much appreciated.

Riechers (2012) offered a cultural and historical perspective on RIP trolling. She pointed out that public mourning is not a new practice, and that RIP sites extend and expand traditions that have been practiced for many years. She reminds us of cultures in which paid professional mourners are hired to attend a funeral (e.g., in ancient Greece and China), with the number of mourners reflecting the importance of the deceased person. In the Victorian era, strangers who were dressed in the clothing and sorrowful mien befitting such a solemn occasion were hired to increase the size of the attendees. New Orleans funerals may end with a jazz band parading through the streets; many people who had no relationship with the departed individual join the parade. Reichers believes that online grieving pages also provide a collective mourning space, while allowing visitors to demonstrate (perhaps to themselves) their sensitive and sympathetic qualities. Online comments on such sites function somewhat like the guest book at a wake or funeral service, expanding that practice to allow one to react to and comment on previous signers' notes.

Riechers (2012) groups visits to RIP pages into four categories: the genuine mourner, grief tourists (no connection to the dead person), trolls, and lurkers (who observe but don't participate). She points out that grief tourists exist in the offline world as well; many people visit concentration camp memorials without knowing anyone who was lost there. The trolls, however, while perhaps attempting to draw attention to the perceived absurdity of grief tourism, create excitement by keeping the dialog (and outrage) alive. In a way, the trolls are mocking not the individual who died, but the social norms and expectations of responding to death in our society. Trolls also highlight the fact that the internet is not the safe place some people naively believe it to be, and believe they are helping people realize that.

In the mainstream media, obituaries are published about famous and ordinary people, but published pieces are edited for content. Online, there is no editor, and thus there is the chance for trolls to set the bait. Moreover, sensational deaths are often reported by the traditional media. I am also reminded of the inevitable traffic snarl when there is a gruesome accident. The emergency services have arrived, the vehicles have been moved so that traffic is not blocked, but still drivers slow down to get a closer look at tragedy. Phillips (2011) points out that the interest in gore creates a symbiotic relationship between trolls and the media: The media publishes a sensational story about a teenage death, trolls find ways to mock the decreased, the media reports their outrageous behaviors, which increases the troll's audience and attention. The media audience (and advertising revenue) is also enhanced by the coverage of the trolls' extreme behaviors, so each platform contributes to the other's goals.

Political Trolls

This discussion begs for a definition of "political," which is, like many topics in this book, somewhat vague and subjective. Aristotle's oft-quoted statement that "man is by nature a political animal" has been interpreted to mean that as a social being that lives in groups, there is a need for structure by which public practices or rules are determined. Aristotle viewed the instruments of government as necessary for organizing society but held that there is also a private arena that does not require government oversight. Of course, delineating the line between public and private spheres is challenging at best, but I use the term *political* in this book to refer to activities, practices, regulations, policies, and roles that relate to the way our society is governed.

Political trolling was apparent in the 2012 American presidential campaign in which political memes were widely used by Obama trolls. Burroughs (2013) stated that although the internet was a factor in 2008, 2012 was the first year a real social media campaign took off. The memes that were circulated portrayed Barack Obama as lacking patriotism. An interesting observation is that whereas long ago, the speed of distribution of a message was a function of the speed of the horse on which the messenger rode, now the messages can be disseminated as soon as it is created. This makes social media a more efficient purveyor of content than mass media (radio and television). The trolls were able to get their memes out before the mass media could, shaping the nature of the discourse. Where in previous times, pamphlets and direct mailings were used to distribute political messages, the digital era facilitates that process and enlarges the size of the potential audience. For example, a false report about death panels that was promoted during the debates about Obamacare claimed a nonexistent doctor and a nonexistent hospital said Obamacare resulted in diminished services, thus causing patient deaths. This particular troll technique is insidious—using what seem to be reliable sources appears to legitimize the content. Unfortunately, even the most discerning readers don't have time to fact-check every item they see, so embedding the messages with such professional-sounding support increases the likelihood they will be accepted as truth.

Political trolling is different from the types of trolling discussed so far in that it is not done for the lulz but is a method of spreading an ideology (Burroughs, 2013). Political trolls use their voices to influence and manipulate public opinion, thereby also potentially influencing the outcome of elections. Most trolls (but not all) originate from the *alt-right*, a term created by Richard Spencer in 2008 to distinguish a right-wing political movement that disagreed with more mainstream conservatism and espoused White nationalism ideology (Marwick & Lewis, 2017). Progressives also practice trolling, though perhaps in a less consistent way (Benko, 2017). Political trolls circulate disinformation, attack candidates they oppose by promoting and sometimes creating false stories, and use extreme language to express their views. Interestingly, because trolls are often sarcastic, when alt-right trolls are challenged, they claim "success"— that is, that their comments were just to lure readers into having a reaction, the raison d'etre for classic trolls.

According to Earle (2017), this practice did not originate with the 2016 election cycle. In fact, he claims that the U.S. government hired the company that owns Cambridge Analytica in 2011 to create fake profiles on social media to circulate political content. Trolls in the political arena may be paid for their work by political parties, organizations, and in some cases, government entities.

The Internet Research Agency is a large government-sponsored organization in St. Petersburg, Russia, whose employees churn out such messages and memes in huge quantities, flooding social media with misleading (at best) content. They also use robots (bots), fake accounts that appear to be real people, to automatically send out massive messaging via social media to sway public opinion. A former employee of the agency (Marat Mindiyarov) was interviewed by J. J. Green in 2018, and described an austere working environment in which employees received e-mail instructions at the beginning of their shifts; the e-mails contained links to websites where comments were to be posted, the topics that were to be the subject of those comments, and the message to be conveyed. The informant reported that information they were directed to post was often clearly false. Before long, Mindiyarov quit the job, finding the whole situation to be Orwellian and too uncomfortable to continue.

The Oxford Internet Institute (OII, of Oxford University in England) studies information and communication technologies. It observed that the 2016 presidential campaign in the United States was a period of significant media manipulation. For example, it found that close to Election Day, fake news was distributed as widely as was professional journalism. Cambridge Analytica was a British consulting firm from 2013 to 2018 that was employed by the Trump campaign to access data on Facebook users that could then be used to create ads targeted at particular profiles. The data that the firm gathered on 50 million Facebook users are a subject of debate, because although the data were at that time available to researchers, the way they were used, and the extent of data obtained is contrary to the policies of the website.

The Trump camp was very proficient at using bots to disseminate messages; Trump-favoring bots generated five times the activity as did the Clinton bots. The bots share or retweet each other's messages and insert ads along with the message content. Overall, Trump's campaign garnered 15% more coverage from mainstream media sources than did Clinton's. Another tactic that the Trump campaign used was targeted messages. For example, a 20-year-old comment by Clinton interpreted to mean she favored mass incarceration of Black males was resurrected and highlighted in trolled messages on Facebook to African Americans during the 2016 campaign.

A study using Twitter data from Russian troll accounts (Stewart, Arif, & Starbird, 2018) adds to our understanding of political trolling. The study focused on the Russian trolls' activities in the heated discussions around gun violence and race relations. It points out that social media consumers tend to read and share content almost exclusively with other users who share their views. The algorithms that determine what content a user sees utilize demographic data as well as the social network information available. Hashtags can also be used to signal the political leaning of a conversation, allowing users to choose topics with which they are sympathetic. In their analysis, Stewart et al. (2018) found that retweets of Russian trolls' posts were more frequent among the left-leaning users than on the right-leaning users, but the troll posts account for a high proportion of retweets on both ends of the political spectrum. They conclude that the trolls infiltrated American accounts to further polarize existing divisions and to spread disinformation and propaganda across all political positions to destabilize the discussions. Trolls are a potent force for manipulating social media that appropriate the nature of social media to their ends. They may also reflect fears of some segments of the population who resist changing social norms (e.g., gay marriage).

Burroughs (2013) chronicles a series of Obama memes that were designed to show he was not only unpatriotic but also insulting to American values. One of the memes showed Obama at Arlington National Cemetery on Veteran's Day; he was not saluting. What was not included in the meme was the information that the photo was taken when "Hail to the Chief" (Obama) was playing, and the president does not salute himself. Another meme showed Obama with his hand over his heart, with the text saying this was during the playing of the Russian national anthem. In reality, it was the American national anthem that was playing. These were widely circulated, particularly among anti-Obama circles. Comments and sharing or retweets spread them to ever-larger audiences, confirming the worst nightmares of those who feared what Obama represented.

Osnos (2016) described the social media fallout from a dispute between Sanders supporters and Clinton supporters at the Nevada Democratic Convention. There was plenty of drama on the convention floor, but the chairperson of the Nevada Democratic Party received a large number of texts (and voicemails) with profanities and threats to rape and kill her, and messages of the "I know where you live, etc." variety. A reporter was able to track down a few of the people who sent these kinds of messages, and Osnos notes that the troll was encouraged by Anonymous (a hacker and troll collective) and playing a role. He also claimed to be disabled, unemployed, and very frustrated.

Lest it seem that only the alt-right and Trump supporters engage in political trolling, a Democratic effort to sway voters in Alabama was discovered (Shane & Blinder, 2019). A group of organized progressive activists created a Facebook page and Twitter feed claiming that the Republican candidate Roy Moore planned to ban alcohol statewide. They also targeted ads on Facebook that presented that falsehood as fact. The trolls believed that the more moderate Republicans would be opposed to such a plan and might vote against Moore. Shane and Blinder note that there is no evidence that the Democratic candidate knew of this operation, nor did he know of another operation, in which they created numerous false Twitter accounts, made to look as if they were Russian trolls, to follow Moore. The Democratic candidate won the election by 22,000 votes out of more than 1.3 million cast. There is no way to determine whether either of the trolling efforts influenced that outcome, but the Facebook posts had 4.6 million views, and 97,000 likes and/or shares; video posts were viewed 430,000 times (Shane & Blinder, 2019).

Shane and Blinder interviewed some of the participants in these episodes. They reported that one of those who worked on these operations said that although he disapproved of these tactics, they were a necessity because they are being so widely used by Republican groups, and another person who funded these efforts said he was concerned "that our tactics might cause us to become like those we are fighting" (2019, paragraph 11).

Political trolling is now a fact of digital life in America, and given the affordances of social media, it is unlikely that this practice will abate. It behooves readers, regardless of their political persuasion, to approach social media with a healthy dose of skepticism.

TOOLS USED BY TROLLS

Memes

Trolls have a penchant for using *memes* to spread their provocative messages. The term was first used by an evolutionary biologist, Richard Dawkins, in 1976 (Jordan, 2014). It is derived from the Greek *mimema*, meaning "something imitated"; the current usage refers to an idea or bit of content that spreads widely through cyberspace. Most often, memes are images that have had a clever caption added. The images are appropriated and often are of people or animals (think cats) that are not inherently associated with the message conveyed in the caption. Memes are designed to spread quickly via social media and are often modified and re-purposed. Thus, most memes are sarcastic or humorous. Trolls believe they originally popularized memes, and the practice has now has gone mainstream (Jussinoja, 2018; Phillips, 2013). Burroughs (2013) quotes Jenkins (2008) who suggests that memes are analogous to editorial cartoons, created by the general population and designed to make a strong visual impression that embodies a particular idea. Jenkins says, "In many cases, they aim lower than what we would expect from an established publication and so they are a much blunter measure of how popular consciousness is working through shifts in the political landscape" (p. 263). There are many websites available to the ordinary citizens to create memes to share on social media.

Pepe the Frog is a notable meme, initially created by artist Matt Furie in 2005 as part of a comic series he created and originally posted on his MySpace page. The comic recounts the mundane experiences of four post-college guys: Pepe the Frog, Brett, Andy, and Landwolf. One panel showed a rear view of Pepe urinating with his pants pulled down to his ankles. When asked about that practice later, Pepe said, "Feels good, man." Roy (2016) described how both the image and the phrase were used and reused, often in altered forms—there are sad Pepes and angry Pepes, and have been widely disseminated on social media sites, including 4chan, Reddit, and Tumblr. Pepe was reblogged on Tumblr more than any other meme in 2015 (Nelson, 2016).

In one incarnation, Pepe wears a Hitler mustache and the tag line is "Kill Jews Man," prompting the Anti-Defamation League (ADL) to designate Pepe as a hate symbol. Pepe was featured in other anti-Semitic memes; Nazi Pepe has been tweeted by White nationalists and anti-immigrant proponents. To the delight of many trolls and Pepe fans, Hillary Clinton referenced Pepe in a speech and Donald Trump Jr. included Pepe in an Instagram photo of a group of Donald Trump supporters. Roy observed that Furie is "devastated" by the transformation of Pepe from an innocuous creature to a symbol of hate. He has since stopped producing the Pepe comic, but he could not resist a "last laugh": He posted on Tumblr a drawing of Pepe wearing a MAGA hat and "urinating on a green-faced Trump" (Roy, 2016, paragraph 26).

Bots

Bots are software algorithms that create content on social media that appear to come from real people (Marwick & Lewis, 2017), and are used by trolls to spread disinformation and to increase the apparent number of followers a person (e.g., candidate) has. Bots can send spam e-mail to hordes of addresses or can flood—and presumably shut down—a website with the large numbers of visitors (Yiu, 2018). The 2016 election campaign online was littered with bots. For example, although bots were less than 0.5% of users who posted about the first debate between Trump and Clinton, they created 20% of the Twitter posts about it, with most bot posts coming from Trump bots. It is quite difficult for most users to recognize when a poster is a bot, so their use is often undetected.

Bots can be hijacked by trolls. Case in point: Microsoft released a bot that was supposed to have conversations and increase its conversational repertoire by interacting in online chats. Unfortunately, it very quickly learned to put out racist and other inappropriate tweets and was shut down in one day. Trolls using bots (some purported to be Russians) disseminated enormous quantities of disinformation about both Christine Blasey Ford and Brett Kavanaugh during the controversy and her testimony to the U.S. Senate (Haldevang, 2018).

Hashtags

Hashtags are used on social media to convey a concise topic so that other users can more easily locate posts with a given theme. Trolls sometimes use these to signal to other trolls so that they can coordinate attacks. They may also use a popular hashtag to lure unsuspecting users to their message, which has nothing to do with the hashtag. This is common in the political arena, where trolls seek to increase attention to their negative messages (Campbell, 2013).

Doxing

Doxing refers to the troll device of finding offline data (address, phone number, job, identification numbers, etc.) of a target and publicizing that on social media. A self-identified troll was suspended by Twitter after doxing Christine Blasey Ford, the woman who testified that Supreme Court nominee Brett Kavanaugh had sexually assaulted her in high school. However, the post was online for several hours and was copied and shared on other social media sites.

FAMOUS (OR INFAMOUS) TROLLS

There are a few characters who are well known for their determined trolling. They appear to thrive on the reactions as trolls do, but they are also promoting an ideology. Mike Cernovich is a blogger and vlogger (video blogs) who actively promotes the alt-right agenda and was the first to circulate the idea that Hillary Clinton was seriously ill (Marantz, 2016). An example of his activities is his handling of one of candidate Clinton's speeches during the campaign. When the speech was announced, Cernovich livestreamed his call to action, giving instructions to his followers. He told his audience that Clinton's illness was severe and disabling, and that the mainstream media were concealing that fact. He urged his audience to tweet about her supposed medical condition and to propagate certain hashtags and memes. He hoped Clinton would attack him in her speech, making himself a trending topic on social media. He said to Marantz, "Conflict is attention. Attention is influence" (paragraph 5, online version). Cernovich also acknowledged that he became a "political commentator" (read "troll") when Trump entered the political arena.

Another well-known troll is Milo Yiannopoulos, who described himself as a "virtuous troll" (Begley, 2017). On the topic of Clinton's health, Yiannopoulos chimed in with anti-Clinton rhetoric the next day. Yiannopoulos worked for alt-right website Breitbart. His posts are often outrageous; his defense of pedophilia sparked strong criticism and resulted in lost speaking engagements and a book contract. (Note: He later self-published the book that became a best seller.) He promotes himself as the world's most controversial man and appears to have no self-regulation mechanism and strives to satirize and expose the hypocrisy he sees in all levels of society. He has been condemned by some and lauded by others for his affinity to neo-Nazi and White supremacist causes and people. Yiannopoulos was permanently banned from Twitter in 2016, but still has a Facebook celebrity page with 2,344,589 followers (January 2019).

Keep in mind that most trolls prefer to be anonymous, so these individuals (and Alex Jones, another social media provocateur) are the exception. What they share with all trolls is the enjoyment of the strong reactions to their activities, the pleasure at the attention, and the disregard of social niceties. Their ideology, their higher purpose, in their minds gives them license to distort or create narratives with no regard for facts.

PLATFORMS FOR TROLLS

Although most have been mentioned earlier in the chapter, I thought it would be useful to briefly review the online platforms that attract trolls.

Twitter

Twitter has always been a popular site for trolls, because it has a large base of subscribers, is easy to navigate, and retweets increase exposure. Trump uses this site as his primary vehicle to publicize his thoughts and opinions. He openly disparages traditional news media, and by using Twitter he avoids oversight or editing of his communiqués by staff or editors. The algorithm that determines what a subscriber sees has been adjusted so that the most aggressive and argumentative tweets achieve prominence. This has increased advertising revenue for Twitter and increased traffic on the site.

A fascinating study published in *Science* in 2018 examined patterns of tweets about true and false news items from 2006 to 2017 (Vosoughi, Roy, & Aral, 2018). Using rigorous methods and validation procedures, the researchers found that false news was distributed more quickly and more widely than true news. Furthermore, false political news was the most viral of all categories of news items. False stories were also more likely to be retweeted. Interestingly, they conducted the analysis with and without with bot-generated messages included, and the outcome was the same. However, the bots affected the distribution of both false and true news equally, so the authors conclude that the profusion of false news spreading on Twitter is a result of human users.

Facebook

Facebook has a huge subscriber base; Statistica reports that Facebook had 2.38 billion monthly active users as of the first quarter of 2019; active users are those who logged on in the previous 30 days. Despite its large audience, Swisher (2018) contends that Facebook is "too bloated and slow," to be useful for Trump, whose frequent tweets are designed for immediate reactions. On the other hand, the character limit on Twitter forces the troll to condense the message, sometimes leading to missing context or important details. Facebook does not have such limits. Facebook is a favorite platform for RIP trolls, as noted earlier.

Reddit

Reddit was an early entry into the social media realm, started in 2005 by two recent college grads. They allowed users to have as many anonymous accounts as they liked; users vote for posts they like (upvote) and those posts then move up to the top of the feed. The creators of the site originally promoted it as a space free of censorship and restrictions, but very soon they decided to label some posts NSFW (not safe for work), intending to keep users from being embarrassed if they opened something not appropriate for the workplace. Reddit was ultimately purchased by a large corporation, the creators left, and the userbase grew. Soon, a known troll created some racist and borderline-illegal (e.g., Jailbait for sexual photos of youthful-looking women who were supposedly over 18) communities known as subreddits. Users of the site protested any effort to control content, which was a damper on the activities of trolls. However, the original creator returned to Reddit as CEO in 2015 and has closed subreddits that encourage hate speech, although they don't close the accounts of individual users. A subreddit called The_Donald (with 500,000 subscribers) was used to promote Trump's candidacy, and to dispute attacks he received on other platforms. As for Reddit, it has a reputation of being particularly noxious and has an acknowledged "dark side." Reddit, along with 4chan, organized and executed a coordinated attack on a female critic of gaming by doxing, engaging in vulgar verbal abuse, and making rape and death threats. The campaign became known as #gamergate, and although 4chan banned that discussion, the movement migrated to 8chan, Reddit, and YouTube.

4chan

4chan started in 2003 as a space for admirers of Japanese anime and manga. It is considered the online home of trolls (Merrin, 2019). Soon after its launch, discussions boards were created on a wide range of topics; the /b/ board is the most popular and is called the "random" board, perhaps because there are almost no constraints on content, and because memes often make their debut here. Marwick and Lewis (2017) report that this board contains offensive language, porn, disgusting images, and hateful posts about women and minorities. 4chan is home to White males, and others should expect to be shocked at the content. The minimal restrictions on content have allowed trolls to create memes and plan and execute attacks on other social media. Its users are anonymous, and if a user declines to fill in the name field for a post, it will show as "Anonymous."

4chan users are known to troll other forums (and are not biased toward any political view), and then brag to the group about his or her successes (the lulz). According to Merrin (2019), politics was not a main function of 4chan, but from 2008 forward it has had a political, mostly left-leaning, faction—Anonymous. While this group continues to have a role, 4chan itself took on a definite alt-right identity. For example, someone in the /pol/ group posted a tongue-in-cheek comment referring to the John Podesta e-mail hack in 2016. The post implied that the word *pizza* found in those e-mails was actually code for pedophilia; another user suggested that the group "meme this into reality" (Merrin, 2019), which they did. They created a bizarre narrative about a child porn ring with ties to Hillary Clinton that was housed in a pizza restaurant in Washington, D.C. These trolls then propagated the story on Twitter, Reddit, and other social media. This troll scheme inspired a person to enter the pizza place with the intent to free the child sex workers, and who fired several shots and held a worker hostage.

Merrin (2019) maintains that the Trump campaign, while not originating some of the messages and memes, retweeted some of these obviously false posts to bias viewers against Clinton. The campaign workers observed which messages were most effective, and then shared those on Facebook.

WHO IS A TROLL?

Personality Studies

Given the disturbing nature of trolling, researchers have sought to identify personality traits that characterize them. Previous studies related to the personalities of socially malicious persons have found that narcissism, psychopathy, and Machiavellianism are found at higher than expected levels in such individuals. The three traits are known as the Dark Triad; recently, a fourth trait, sadism, has been identified and the new group is called the Dark Tetrad (Craker & March, 2016).

A relatively early study on this topic (Buckels, Trapnell, & Paulhus, 2014) examined the Dark Tetrad in their sample of 418 U.S. adults. In the sample, 5.6% reported their preferred online activity was trolling; this group had the highest scores on the Dark Tetrad personality traits. The researchers then conducted a follow-up study with 609 U.S. adults and 188 Canadian college students. Participants with high scores on the Dark Tetrad commented more frequently on interactive sites. Looking more closely at their data, the researchers found that sadism and Machiavellianism predicted enjoyment of trolling, but sadism had the strongest association; psychopathy was unrelated to trolling, and narcissism was negatively related so that the more narcissism, the less enjoyment of trolling. Buckels et al. suggest that opportunities to be a troll might be uniquely suitable for those with sadistic traits, who find pleasure in the suffering of others.

Craker and March (2016) investigated the presence of this personality constellation in internet trolls and also studied the motivations that propel trolls. They surveyed 396 adults who had active Facebook accounts and found that Facebook trolls have low levels of empathy, are callous, and take pleasure from others' pain. They are motivated by attaining power and influence over others, albeit in a negative way (embarrassing or enraging others).

Another study investigated similar variables, this time on dating apps (March, Grieve, Marrington, & Jonason, 2017). They investigated the Dark Tetrad and impulsivity to further our understanding of internet trolls and included age and sex in their analyses of data from 357 adults recruited online. The vast majority of participants (90%) used Tinder at the time of the survey. No sex differences were found for trolling, but females in this study reported more trolling behaviors than was the case when the samples were recruited from forums, gaming sites, or Facebook. They found that psychopathy, sadism, and dysfunctional impulsivity were predictors of trolling; further analyses showed that dysfunctional impulsivity was only associated with trolling in those who had high levels of psychopathy.

Interested in comparing personality traits of cyberbullies and trolls, Zezulka and Siegfried-Spellar (2016) recruited 308 adults, of whom 70 acknowledged only cyberbullying behaviors, 20 who only trolled others, 129 who engaged in both forms of digital aggression, and 89 who engaged in neither form. The researchers discovered that those who admitted to more cyberbullying behaviors, but did not troll, had lower scores on neuroticism (emotional instability), while those who trolled and did not cyberbully had higher scores on openness to experience. Openness to experience includes being unconventional, more emotionally expressive, more humorous, and less offended by violations of social norms. Although all the studies described earlier have methodological weaknesses (e.g., small, unrepresentative samples), they shed light on trolling—a behavior that has vexed many and continues to do so.

Is Donald Trump a Troll?

"After all, the man in control of the press conference was the world's most gifted media troll, the President of the United States" (Marantz, 2016). Dockray (2018) refers to Trump as "troll-in-chief" (paragraph 6). Cillizza (2018) observed that the president is now "embracing his inner troll" (paragraph 2), using social media (Twitter) to provoke reactions from others, get media to cover his tweets, spread disinformation, and use memes (often borrowed from the alt-right catalog). He often retweets comments from alt-right commentators. Paul Ryan, when he was Speaker of the House, said of a statement by Trump: "I think he's just trolling people, honestly." @realDonaldTrump has 57 million followers (January 6, 2018), and most are covered and discussed by other media, so if in fact he is a troll, he should be feeling lots of lulz. Merrin (2019) contends that the way Trump uses Twitter "trolls his own administration and the US government system" (p. 213). I would add that he also trolls the mainstream media. An example was a video meme in which he is wrestling an opponent whose head was a CNN logo; the hashtag was #FraudNewsCNN.

If we refer to the beginning of the chapter and the definition of a troll, it is unlikely that Trump meets the criteria. However, I think it is safe to say that his behavior on social media, where he has a very visible presence, consists of a considerable amount of trolling.

EFFORTS TO CONTROL TROLLS

Almost anywhere you look for insight on how to control trolls will include the catchphrase "Don't feed the trolls." The thinking is that since trolls are seeking a reaction or success that requires a response from other users, depriving them of this audience reaction will remove the reward and lead to the disillusionment of the trolls. That is probably good advice, but it is unlikely to eliminate trolling entirely.

In our review of some of the sites where trolls tend to hang out, it is clear that if you seek to avoid trolls, avoiding those sites is essential. 4chan—especially the /b/ and /pol/ boards—would be off-limits to troll-resisters, as would Reddit. The other sites are likely to include some trolls and trolling behaviors, but the frequency and toxicity is generally lower.

Reporting trolling activity that violates the website's terms of use is another action an individual can take. As we have seen, some sites are reluctant to censor content, but most have recognized the need to do so at some level. Reporting as often as necessary to get the material down will get the attention of the people in a position to remove content and or suspend or expel participants.

The most obvious solution is to moderate content on these sites. Most sites do employ human and bot moderators that search posts for words that could point to content that violates their terms of use. While these are useful efforts, the volume of posts makes it unlikely that a significant portion of trolled content will be removed. It appears that individual users will have to decide what they are willing to view and hide or unfriend or otherwise remove trolls from their accounts.

Joshua Cuevas's Story

"The university has become a political minefield" (Shrecker, 2018). Although faculty at public institutions are universally cautioned to refrain from espousing political opinions in their classrooms, conservatives such as Ben Shapiro (2010) maintain that American universities are excessively liberal and seek to brainwash young students with liberal ideology. A 2018 survey by Pew Research (Brown, 2018) found that among Republicans with a negative view of higher education's direction, 79% believe that the problem is that professors use their position to promote their political and social views, presumably to brainwash impressionable young minds. (Only 17% of Democrats shared that view.)

A Prelude

Academia is far from a safe haven from digital aggression, as we have noticed elsewhere in this book. It's important to keep in mind that although social media is a common digital tool for attacking others, e-mail is alive and well and an absolute necessity for academics, who receive important information (along with much unimportant information) and send collaborative work back and forth using that vehicle. An example of how that can be misused is a situation that occurred in a large American university where X, a full professor with an impressive CV, was hired to join the faculty. Both this professor and her husband were accomplished scholars with a reputation for quality work. In the first year after her arrival at the new university, the scholar's husband inadvertently offended someone in her program. The husband was in an administrative position, and thus perceived as untouchable by junior faculty. The offended individual chose to attack X instead. His method of choice was e-mail.

Although the e-mails were addressed to X, a variety of individuals (department heads, deans, upper administration, etc.) were copied. The e-mails did not directly accuse X of misdeeds at first, but used many politically correct buzzwords and implied that X was not a positive colleague or instructor. The e-mails were very lengthy and wordy, designed to paint a picture of a new hire that was not a good fit for the department or college in which she was placed. When X requested a face-to-face meeting, her bully did not respond, but continued to send more e-mails. X followed the protocol at the university for reporting such events. The dean of her college was sympathetic to her plight to the extent that he cautioned the offender to leave her alone. The e-mails did stop, but the offender continued to work behind the scenes to malign X. She feels her trust in the system was undermined, and that the university is unable or unwilling to protect her. Thus, without social media, without embarrassing images, without texts, and others, e-mail was employed to attack and undermine a reputable scholar.

The Story

With such a climate in mind, the experience of Joshua A. Cuevas, a tenured associate professor at the University of North Georgia, is an example of the lengths some people will go to undermine what they perceive to be the "liberal" agenda (see Cuevas, 2018, at https://www.aaup.org/article/ new-reality-far-rights-use-cyberharassment-against-academics#.XGBkX7 h7nIU). The digital aggression began when Cuevas commented on a Facebook post from www.bigthink.com about the electoral college. This topic received increased attention following the 2016 presidential election in which the candidate with the most popular votes did not win the office. For some reason, his comment attracted the attention of a troll (Cuevas calls him troll #1) whose replies seemed to be directed at Cuevas rather than at the topic of debate, and whose posts included personal insults and profanity. This is a logical fallacy known as an "ad hominem" attack.

Consistent with the mantra "don't feed the trolls," Cuevas blocked this troll to avoid further exposure to his nastiness and exited the conversation where the troll had attacked.

Cuevas used his knowledge of technology, social media, and writing to recognize when this same troll took on a different identity to contact him again, posing as a female student. Troll #1 let Cuevas know that he had turned to 4chan—the community of trolls—to enlist others to join his mission to harm Cuevas, telling him "This is going to be bad for you" (paragraph 4, aaup.org). Troll #1's posse attacked with racial slurs, other pejorative labels, scurrilous comments about Cuevas's daughter and others. Cuevas reported:

> People with whom I had never had previous contact began to send me messages. One of the first said, "You're a nigger." Another called me a "faggott" [*sic*]. One attacked my preteen daughter as illegitimate. Several other individuals, including a person who identified himself on his personal page as being employed as a data scientist at Facebook, used the phrase, "You must go back." I did not initially understand what he meant by this but quickly came to realize that he was implying that, because I am Hispanic, I should be deported. (Paragraph 4, aaup.org)

Given the nature of the comments, Cuevas believes he was targeted because he represented the academy (elite educated liberals) and a minority group (Hispanics), both of which are perceived to be threats by the alt-right. It was also obvious that false accounts were created specifically for committing these anonymous attacks; some of the abusers posed as students or parents to make the accusations seem more widespread. The devious trolls also found Cuevas's RateMyProfessors page and posted fake disparaging comments about his teaching, including many false and inflammatory statements about his methods and his assignments, with the goal of having Cuevas dismissed from the university.

Cuevas learned that groups on 4chan provide training sessions on how to disrupt a conversation and sow discord online. Despite the many attacks of which he was aware, Cuevas learned from one of his own students that there were even more racist, vulgar attacks on an alt-right website that were so harsh the student felt compelled to alert Cuevas. Discussions on that site were openly planning malicious and devious strategies, including altering comments made on the original discussion and making it appear that they were made by Cuevas, using racial epithets, invoking images of Hitler and other nefarious symbols, portraying Cuevas as an anti-Semite, attempting to discredit his research and scholarship. At one point, a message that appeared to come from a student was sent to 77 members of the college faculty, accusing Cuevas of using his teaching to espouse anti-Semitism. By this time, Cuevas had alerted his superiors that this campaign to discredit him was under way; he provided them with screen-shots and other documentation of the online assault; they recommended he pursue criminal charges. After another onslaught of aggressive messages, and the removal of the fraudulent RateMyProfessors comments and close monitoring of the ratings, the activity finally waned.

That was not the end of the digital aggression, however. Five months later, someone created a fake e-mail message that to students appeared to come from Cuevas. The message contained a bogus final exam, which was to write a critical essay about Trump, cautioning that those with pro-Trump essays would be penalized. A copy of the e-mail was sent to Cuevas's department head in a renewed attempt to disparage his integrity as a professor. This fabricated message heralded a new wave of attacks, many in the form of e-mails to Cuevas with shockingly vicious rhetoric. In addition to 4chan, Reddit and a site called Rtrump were involved in the campaign, and Facebook was also used. Screenshots were altered to insinuate that Cuevas was posting strongly partisan content online, and these were disseminated to a broad audience of students, parents, colleagues, administrators. Cuevas recognized that these messages were written by the same small group of aggressors; their writing contained recognizable patterns.

During this period, Cuevas heard from 70 professors, 20 of whom shared that they had also been targeted using digital media. Nevertheless, Cuevas knew that many who received these messages and viewed the content of websites with reprehensible posts falsely attributed to him fell for the plot and believed that Cuevas was engaging in unprofessional (and extremist) behavior. Evidence of the far-reaching influence of the digital aggression is in the actions taken by a state senator (who contacted Cuevas about the supposed activity) and a U.S. congressman who contacted the university.

Cuevas expressed some disappointment about the university's tepid official response to the allegations they received. Individual faculty members and administrators expressed strong support, but the university as an institution did not make a blanket statement clarifying that the attackers were a small group of White supremacists, and that student harassment of professors would not be tolerated.

It is noteworthy that about three months after the second wave of attacks, the shameful incident at Charlottesville, Virginia, occurred. Cuevas is concerned that the same extremists (and their ilk) who orchestrated that digital attacks on him are emboldened to make such public and physical displays of their beliefs. He decries the temperate nature of academia's response to the rise of these dangerous philosophies, perhaps to shield themselves from charges of being too liberal. Cuevas believes that the danger to our country is severe and that the voices of the academy should not be silenced.

In addition to the impact on Cuevas, this story is an illustration of the extent to which alt-right trolls will go to harass and disrupt the life of a target. In this case, they made not only threats about his family but also serious efforts to get him dismissed from the university. As far as he knows, Cuevas did not have any personal relationship with the anonymous trolls, so it is likely their choice of target was random, selecting someone based on a post with which they disagreed and his ethnicity and position. This chilling scenario reminds us that anyone can be victimized by these trolls who derive pleasure from the misery they inflict. The original incident occurred on Facebook, which is not a specifically political space, and it is one that many adults frequent. The political climate in which we live is rife with division and anger that appears to have found spaces (e.g., 4chan) where this kind of malicious behavior is encouraged.

Frances Lynch's Story

Symbols are powerful images that evoke strong emotional reactions in those for whom the symbol has meaning. For Frances Lynch's father, who lived through the bombings in London during World War II, the Berlin Wall is a symbol of the loss of freedom and human rights. He felt so strongly about the devastating consequences of war and fascism that he instilled in his eldest daughter the importance of understanding history and speaking out for freedom and basic human values. He and his family eventually left England and came first to Canada and then to the United States, where Frances is a citizen.

As the Berlin Wall is a symbol of division and authoritarianism, the wall on the U.S. border with Mexico is also a symbol, representing the need to control immigration from the South (there is no call for a wall on the border with Canada). For many who live near the border, this wall represents a dehumanization of our southern neighbors, and impedes the flow of trade, commerce, tourism, and contact with family and friends.

A border wall has existed in Nogales (Arizona and Sonora, Mexico) since 1918, with four international ports of entry to administer cross-border traffic. Citizens of both countries frequently cross the border for medical care, shopping, or visiting friends and families. Recently, as a result of Trump's insistence that a fortified barrier is necessary, U.S. troops added rows and rows of razor wire covering the wall with as many as six rolls of wire (see Rosenberg, 2019 for an image). To many this is the picture that evoked the Berlin Wall, presenting an image of a place at war or a maximum-security prison.

Frances Lynch, an attorney in Tucson, Arizona, is a fellow of the OpEd Project (https://www.theopedproject.org/), which trains, encourages, and supports women who are experts and leaders in a variety of fields to ensure their voices are heard by a wide audience. For Lynch, given her upbringing and her geographic proximity to the wall, the razor wire addition to the Nogales wall was a made-to-order topic for her to write about, and her opinion piece, critical of the razor wire, was published by *USA Today* on November 26, 2018. Although Lynch was aware that comments on such pieces might not all be laudatory, she did not anticipate the volume and degree of animosity in the comments, nor did she expect the phone calls and e-mails that also arrived. As is common in these cases, many of the comments on Twitter and elsewhere attacked Lynch as a person—her maturity, her intelligence, her patriotism, her gender ("this is why women should not have the right to vote") rather than her views on the topic under discussion.

Furthermore, another online media site, realclearpolitics.com, also posted her story, which added to the exposure and consequently to the barrage of criticism. Keep in mind that for the media, whether print or online, views of content affect the bottom line, so pieces that garner attention of any kind are good news. Lynch was advised by her mentor in the OpEd project not to read the hate comments, but to have someone else do so in case there was a credible threat that needed action. Her mentor contacted people at *USA Today* and realclearpolitics.com to alert them to the nature of the attacks. For example, among the messages Lynch received, there was a phone call threatening professional retaliation if she reported the harassment, and unsubtle comments about the locks on her doors, strongly implying she was not safe anywhere. Although neither organization took any action to remove the comments or post a general caution about using threatening language on their sites, Lynch realized that these are the risks of speaking out in today's digital world, risks that surely stifle less confident voices.

Although the experience of digital aggression upset Lynch, she believes she was better able to weather such attacks because she had previously worked as a criminal defense lawyer, also an unpopular position, and so had been inoculated against threats and opprobrium. She is trained in the martial arts, keeps wasp spray handy (it is quite toxic and propels a fair distance), and is generally savvy about self-protection.

As she continues her experience in the OpEd project, Lynch expects to write additional pieces—about insurance law, her area of expertise and current practice. She commented that she did not think articles on that topic would be controversial, but in the current digital climate, I would not bet the farm that there would be no hostile or vitriolic reactions to future pieces regardless of the topic.

7

Revenge Porn, Slut Shaming, and #MeToo

THE CONTEXT

According to the U.S. Census Bureau, 50.8% of the U.S. population is female. At the same time, only 23.4% of members of the U.S. House of Representatives are female, as are 25% of U.S. senators. Nine of 50 governors of U.S. states are women—and these are historic highs. In 2016, we had the first woman presidential nominee of a major political party.

The Equal Rights Amendment, first passed by Congress in 1972, requires ratification by three-fourths (38) of the states. At the time of this writing, only 37 states had ratified it, so the Twenty-Seventh Amendment to the U.S. Constitution—that says, in part: "Equality of rights under the law shall not be denied or abridged by the United States or by any state on account of sex,"—has yet to become the part of the Constitution. Note that even if the 38th state ratifies it, there was a 1982 deadline for ratification that has not been revised, so there would likely be legal issues to resolve (theoretically simple) before it would be final.

In addition to the inability to get enough states to grant women equal legal status in the Constitution, there has been a recent surge in efforts to restrict access to abortion, another issue of great importance to women. New laws in Mississippi, Alabama, Louisiana, and Georgia, if they withstand court challenges, will make it almost impossible for women in those states to get a legal abortion. Recently, several states have imposed "heartbeat" laws that prohibit abortion after a fetal heartbeat can be detected.[1] Since the start of a pregnancy is typically measured from the date of the woman's most recent menstrual period, that effectively means legal abortion would be prohibited at two weeks following the missed period, when many women might not yet know they are pregnant. Some states make allowances for later abortions when the pregnancy is the result of rape or incest, or if the woman's life is at risk. Georgia's HB481, signed by the governor in May 2019, also allows women who are convicted of getting an illegal abortion to be sentenced to life in prison or death.

Related to these issues, we observe that nine U.S. congressmen have been accused of sexual misconduct and resigned (or did not seek reelection for office) as a result (Cranley, 2018). Many credit the willingness of women to come forward with these allegations to the #MeToo movement. I will look more closely at the #MeToo movement later in the chapter.

Why do I mention these things here? Women's issues, such as having a voice in government, having equal rights, reproductive rights, being safe from sexual abuse and assault, are current political issues that are prominent in our national discourse. It is likely that the 2020 elections will include more women candidates than previous elections. The way in which digital media have been used to damage women (in the case of revenge porn and slut shaming) is important to examine, and the counterpoint—the #MeToo hashtag and movement—demonstrates the power of social media to make changes and influence the political arena.

> The way in which digital media have been used to damage women (in the case of revenge porn and slut shaming) is important to examine, and the counterpoint—the #MeToo hashtag and movement—demonstrates the power of social media to make changes and influence the political arena.

The *Oxford Dictionary* defines revenge porn as "Revealing or sexually explicit images or videos of a person posted on the Internet, typically by a former sexual partner, without the consent of the subject and in order to cause them distress or embarrassment" and slut shaming as "stigmatizing or disparaging a woman for engaging in behavior that is judged to violate social norms regarding sexuality. Often the object of slut shaming is presented as promiscuous or sexually provocative." Poole (2014) says, "Slut-shaming is the act or idea of attacking a female for being sexual" (p. 231). Revenge porn is sometimes considered a subtype of slut shaming.

A STORY

So, I begin with a story. I did not interview the story's protagonist—Monica Lewinsky—for this book, but I did attend her keynote presentation at the International Bullying Prevention Association annual meeting, met her briefly, and have read all the articles she has written, as well as articles written by others about her situation, and viewed *Monica in Black and White* and her 2015 Ted Talk. I chose to anchor this chapter with this particular story because although the scandal occurred pre-social media,[2] it has recently received renewed attention, perhaps due to the #MeToo movement and Lewinsky's decision to use her voice to call attention to the problem. This gives us a chance to view an example of slut shaming that spans the evolution of the digital universe, and to consider a case that had a wide national exposure.

If the number of people who view an item on social media is a measure of the severity of the incident, consider that from January 1998 to February 1999, a total of almost 40 hours of air time was spent reporting on the scandal by the three major TV networks at the time (ABC, CBS, NBC) (Waxman & Fabry, 2018). Barron and Hoban (1998) were tongue-in-cheek appalled that updates on the story even interrupted their favorite soap opera! Without knowing the size of the viewership of those news shows, it's safe to conclude that this story had unprecedented national coverage. In fact, the scandal was also called "Monicagate, Lewinskygate, Sexgate, and zippergate" (Barron & Hoban, 1998) to suggest it was as monumental as Watergate, the scandal that led to President Nixon's resignation. Lewinsky reports that in a single newspaper (the *Washington Post*) 125 articles about this scandal were published in the first 10 days from the first coverage, attesting to the wide exposure of this case. She also observes that despite the 20 years that have elapsed since this occurred, there has been at least one reference in the press every single day since (Lewinsky, 2018).

The following chronology of the slut-shaming incident is based primarily on a *Time* magazine article by Waxman and Fabry (2018). In 1995, Monica Lewinsky, a 21-year-old unpaid intern at the White House, began a two-year affair with Bill Clinton, then president of the United States. In 1998, independent counsel Kenneth Starr was investigating some real estate investments by the Clintons when he received tape recordings of telephone conversations in which Monica confided about the affair to Linda Tripp, whom she considered a close friend.

Although Monica initially signed an affidavit (in a separate court case against Clinton) that she had not had a sexual relationship with the president, the tape recordings contradicted that statement. On January 17, 1998, the *Drudge Report* (an online news aggregator site) reported on a tip about the affair, which Clinton denied. Several days later, *Drudge* additionally reported that Monica had kept a blue dress with the president's dried semen, although this had not yet been confirmed by DNA analysis of the material on the dress. The story of the blue dress was widely covered in the traditional media. Note that on August 17, after lab testing of a sample of

Clinton's blood, the FBI concluded that the odds that the semen on the dress were *not* from Clinton were 7.87 trillion to 1.

On January 26, President Clinton said on television what has now become an oft-repeated epigram of that affair: *"I did not have sexual relations with that woman, Monica Lewinsky"* (italics added). In May, Monica's lawyer agreed to allow a photographer from *Vanity Fair* to do a photo shoot of her, hoping that the photos would improve her self-esteem, which had been hurt by all the publicity. In June the magazine published an issue containing the glamour photos that "does not go over well in the court of public opinion" (Waxman & Fabry, 2018, paragraph 24). On August 17, Clinton testified before the grand jury and then admitted to "inappropriate intimate contact" with Monica and proclaimed responsibility for his behavior. Then independent counsel Starr released his report, first to Congress and then to the public. Shortly thereafter, the transcripts of the telephone conversations were also made available. In October, the House of Representatives voted to recommend an impeachment inquiry. Interestingly, polls taken at this time showed Clinton's popularity among voters was high and that most opposed the impeachment hearings and did not want Clinton to resign. On December 11 and 12, the House Judiciary committee recommended impeachment (and the House voted to impeach), but Clinton said he would not resign. On February 12, 1999, Clinton was acquitted of the impeachment charges. Monica was not the subject of legal action but was slut-shamed and humiliated very publicly.

Whether it is the 20th anniversary of the hearings or the rise of the #MeToo movement that has focused current attention on Lewinsky's story, interest has been regenerated and Monica's willingness to discuss it publicly has been welcomed. A new docuseries, *The Clinton Affair*, includes extensive material and interviews with Monica, and focuses on Clinton's behavior as well as hers. The notable contrast is that while Monica was relentlessly slut-shamed, Clinton's approval ratings increased. That is, when famous people engage in sexual liaisons that become public, it is almost always the woman who is treated as blameworthy and immoral, while the man is either an addendum to the story or is admired for his virility.

Lewinsky reported that she was devastated by the experience, was depressed for years, and sought therapy for PTSD and depression. She said, "I was branded as a tramp, tart, slut, whore, floozy and of course 'that woman,'" she said. "I was seen by many, known by few" (Kelly, 2018). Currently she is an outspoken anti-bullying advocate who writes and speaks about the events in order to demonstrate that one can recover from even such a monumental case of slut shaming. On the one hand, she says she is relieved that this did not occur in the age of social media, but on the other, she has said that if social media were available at the time, she believes she would have received messages of support that would have helped. I suggest that to find the supportive statements would have required wading through boatloads of derogatory and pejorative comments. Case in point: The *USA Today* article published in 2018, 20 years after "Monicagate," allowed online readers to post comments. Although there were several comments expressing compassion for her suffering (e.g., "She's paid her dues and has tried to move forward in a positive manner. Leave the woman alone") and others proclaiming that shaming is a useful tool for society to enforce social norms, many others continued the slut-shaming narrative: for example, "s**ts earn their shame"; "Monica Lewinsky is an attention-loving slut, plain and simple"; "she made her bed, now sleep in it tramp"; "she's a fuxin whore period. Nothing else nothing better in other words she is TRASH." I wonder if Monica reads these and is finding the support she thought social media would offer.

SLUT SHAMING

Slut shaming was not invented by or for the internet. In fact, Webb (2015) reports on slut-shaming practices during the Roman Republic (BCE), and the intention was the same as it arguably is in the present era: "the cultural suppression of female sexuality." However, the internet and social media offer affordances that vastly increase the reach of slut-shaming incidents, and because it is primarily a women's issue, it merits our attention in this chapter.

A major incident of online slut shaming, *The Fappening*, occurred on August 31, 2014 (Lawson, 2018). A group of hackers had collected private nude photos of female celebrities and posted them on AnonIB, which is a place for users to post pornography. The photos were soon available on 4chan and Reddit, and the event was widely covered by the media. Lawson believes that the discourse around the photos more often supported the women who were exposed and attacked the "patriarchal power structures" (p. 48) that affect treatment of women online. Thinking back to our chapter on online personas, Lawson discussed the need for celebrities to appear authentic and intimate, and such photos as these that were intended to be private satisfy the desires of fans to become close to the celebrity.

In her analysis of media coverage of this event, Lawson (2018) concluded that most coverage (on *Gawker, Buzzfeed, Slate, Perez Hilton, Celebitchy,* and *Variety*) of the hacking incident saw the celebrities as sympathetic victims. The tone of the articles was such that the damage done to the women elicited sympathy from readers. Other coverage criticized articles that blamed the women for having taken such photos. There were articles that noted that no males were targeted, and referred to broader societal issues of sexism. Since iCloud was the source of the photos, many articles discussed security around that and other sites, and speculated on what could be done to improve it. One columnist claimed that celebrities are generally narcissists who like to be looked it, implying that the celebrities would not be shamed by the posting of the photos but rather pleased to receive the attention. In Perez Hilton's coverage of the event, he included the images in his initial post. The response was significant and negative. He removed the images and then apologized in a YouTube video, in which he thanks his readers for criticizing his decision. Not all the targets accepted his apology, with one of the targets, actress Jennifer Lawrence, saying he removed the photos because of the negative reaction, not because he sincerely regretted his error. Many commentators painted the hackers as sexually deviant, and descried the ease with which such people can exploit the affordances of the internet.

The year 2014 also was when the famous #Gamergate incident occurred, in which three women (Anita Sarkeesian, Zoe Quinn, and Brianna Wu) were attacked online and Wu was slut-shamed. The details of the incident are complex, and beyond the scope of this chapter. Suffice it to say that the online gaming industry had been male-dominated from its inception, and it is women who entered the field who were targeted. Zoe Quinn's treatment was horrific, and appeared to be planned and coordinated on message boards on 4chan, 8chan, and Reddit. Quinn is a game developer who developed a game—*Depression Quest*—that was different from most online games in that it was not aggressive or competitive, but was based on a series of interactive scenarios. Although the game garnered favorable reviews in the gaming media, many long-time gamers were highly critical. Then Quinn's ex-boyfriend posted a blog about her that among other things claimed the positive media reviews were penned by Nathan Grayson (a game reviewer) in exchange for sexual favors. As it turned out, Grayson had not authored the review of her game and had mentioned her only in an article published before they met. The slut-shamer Eron Gjoni also doxed Quinn, so that she felt she had to leave her home for safety reasons. Attacks by others followed and included hacking of her social media accounts, sending nude photos to colleagues, calling her father with slut-shaming accusations, and other frightening threats of rape and murder. Both Sarkeesian and Wu were the recipients of severe digital aggression, including doxing and threats, but did not experience having nude or sexual images circulated.

Women who enter the political arena are at risk for cyberaggression, including slut shaming. Telford (2018) reported that a global survey of female legislators revealed that over 40 percent had experienced the wide disseminating of sexual or humiliating content. In 2012, Krystal Ball, a Democrat, was running for Congress in Virginia when a six-year-old party photo that someone located on Facebook, showed Ball in a sexy costume in a compromising situation; there was a man dressed as Rudolph the Red-Nosed Reindeer with a red penis prop on his nose. Ball and others were shown fellating the nose (Fisher, 2012) and, predictably, the photos were posted on national media. The intent clearly was to slut shame her, but in this case, her response foiled the plot and perhaps modeled for other women how one might retain control of the narrative. Although she was encouraged by some advisors to stay out of the public light, or to deny that the photo was of her, she chose to take a stand (Telford, 2018). Courtney (n.d.) posted remarks by Ball, which I include here:

> My biggest support during this whole sad episode of my life has come from supporters of Hillary Clinton. In effect, they have been telling me that what happened to me could have happened to one of their daughters. They will not see their daughters called whores when they run for office just because of some college or post-college party. They will not watch the tide of everything they fought for washed away by the public exposure of female sexuality. Once again, like the heroes that they were a generation ago when they made their careers, they are stepping up to protect young women like me and to support us and to help us to grow up. We are young women. And we are dedicated to serving this country. And we will run for office. And we will win. (paragraph 1)

To counter the slut shaming, Ball did interviews and wrote an Op-Ed for the *Huffington Post,* in which she attacks those who attempted to slut-shame her. Unfortunately, she lost the election, but has gone on to have a career in media and has heard from many women that her forthright response was a model for others.

More recently, a similar incident occurred with a mayoral candidate for reelection in Sonoma, California: Rachel Hundley (Telford, 2018). Someone created a website called Rachel Hundley Exposed that took issue with some of Hundley's decisions as mayor, but also included photos found on her social media. These included some of her photos in her underwear working at the Burning Man festival. Rather than take a passive approach to the smears on the website, Handley created a video that she posted on YouTube and criticized the website owner (who was anonymous) for attempting to slut-shame and scare her. She said that she was not ashamed and did not withdraw.

Slut shaming has already entered the national political arena, however circumspectly. In December 2017, Trump tweeted about female senator Kirsten Gillibrand, who was part of a group of congresswomen who called for the investigation of accusations of sexuality impropriety by Trump. He tweeted, in part "[she] would come to my office 'begging' for campaign contributions not so long ago (and would do anything for them) is now in the ring fighting against Trump." He refuted that he was implying that she offered sexual favors in exchange for campaign contributions, but many lawmakers agreed that the sexual meaning and slut-shaming implication was clear.

REVENGE PORN

Revenge porn refers to the use of nude or sexual images that were originally created and sent to an intimate partner, who later decides to post them publicly to extract revenge, usually following a breakup of the relationship. There are and have been numerous websites that specialize in hosting these images, including identifying information (e.g., name, e-mails, addresses) about the subject (called *doxing* in net-speak) provided by the person posting the images. One study cited by Bates (2017) found that over 50% of 1,244 revenge porn survivors said the images of them included their full names and links to their social media profiles, and 20% reported that their e-mail addresses and phone numbers were also provided.

It is important to understand that these sites are a profitable business enterprise, almost always owned by men, dedicated to damaging the reputation of women. Some sites contact the subject of the images and offer to remove them—for a fee—or refer them to a reputation management service that is often owned by the same people (Langlois & Slane, 2017). Lest the reader think that owners of such sites should be prosecuted, I refer to the 1996 law, known as the Communications Decency Act, that contains section 230: **"No provider or user of an interactive computer service shall be treated as the publisher or speaker of any information provided by another information content provider"** (47 U.S.C. § 230). Effectively, a website owner is not responsible for what is posted by someone else on their site. While some revenge porn site owners have been convicted of crimes, those convictions were the result of other infractions. Furthermore, suing a website owner is not a realistic strategy for most women who have been harmed by this form of digital aggression.

The first revenge porn website, isanyoneup.com was created in 2010 by Hunter Moore (Bates, 2017). In a three-month period in 2011, the site received 10,000 photo submissions and advertising revenue of up to $13,000 per month. The site was eventually sold, but others were created. To help us understand how revenge porn is a money-making operation, Langlois and Slane (2017) examined a U.S.-based revenge porn site myex.com. At the time of their study, the home page of the site showed the most recent posts first and included a title created by the poster (who is anonymous), the name and location of the target, a caption, and one of the photos. If viewers want to see more pictures, there is a mechanism to do so easily. Also included are comments from viewers, which can be extremely pernicious and vulgar. The comments included in the sample reflected disgust, objectification of the target as a porn purveyor, insults, and judgments about body parts. Interestingly, the comments are often also negative toward the poster, referring to his sexual inadequacy, or blaming him for the target's purported offenses (e.g., she cheated because he was unable to satisfy her needs).

Because of the personal information included, targets may receive messages that include threats in addition to shaming and demeaning remarks; the identifying information increases the likelihood that persons the target knows offline (employers, friends, teachers) may see the posts. Although theoretically there is no obstacle to there being male targets, these researchers (Langlois & Slane, 2017) found 1 male target and 19 females. That is to say, most revenge porn is designed to target women—and to make a profit from doing so.

There are a variety of ways in which owners of revenge porn sites make money from this activity (Langlois & Slane, 2017). The sites work to build up a critical mass of information that attracts viewers, whose traffic can then be directed elsewhere. That is, the number of viewers is large because of content posted by others (not the owner of the site), who then has little expense for gaining visitors to the site. Myex.com, according to the researchers, uses Google Analytics and advertising.com along with Ero-Advertising. The first two helps the site match ads that are likely to appeal to the users, and the last pays the owner for directing viewers to their porn websites. The trackers access an enormous amount of information about users—which pages they visit, how long they spend on specific sites, what devices they use to access the site. The goal is to send viewers to the porn sites that charge a fee, unlike the revenge porn site itself, which does not.

It is worth noting that myex.com's terms of use clearly state that users will not invade the privacy of another person, and that they will obtain written consent from anyone whose name or image is used on the site. These terms have not been enforced, unless the target who contacts them is under 18, which would make the site at risk for child pornography offenses. The post includes a button next to it for "remove my name," but takes the subject to a form that is typically not honored according to the researchers. At one time, the same button took the subject to a reputation restoration service that of course charged a fee to assist (Langlois & Slane, 2017).

What is most disturbing is what happens when an image and identifying information is located by Google search engine, which is constantly crawling the web for new data. When it finds the post with the victim's information, it then associates those pages with all other pages that have the target's name. Then, it ranks the traffic on various sites in order of frequency of visits, and lists those at the top of Google search results. Since revenge porn websites have high traffic, the site can be listed near the top. For example, in October 2015, the researchers conducted Google searches on the first 10 names of women featured on myex.com that week (Langlois & Slane, 2017). For eight of them, myex.com was among the first 10 sites listed. This also means that even if the target is successful at getting those images removed from the site, they may already have been spread across other sites, complicating the process. Some women targeted by revenge porn have reported that their images were found on porn sites years later. Services that provide reputation management for a fee have a vested interest in keeping the sites and posts alive. Recently, Google agreed to remove links to revenge porn sites upon request. In the United States, this is a voluntary practice on its part, whereas in other countries, laws have been passed to require such cooperation.

One might think revenge porn occurs only in the denizens of social misfits or angry spurned lovers, but politicians are not immune for the behavior— or the consequences. In August 2018, Illinois representative Nick Sauer resigned after the target of his revenge porn spoke up. Kate Kelly, Sauer's former girlfriend, told police that Sauer had created a fake Instagram account that included nude images of her (without her knowledge or consent). She sent the photos to him during their two-year relationship, which had ended earlier that summer. The editorial board of the *Chicago Tribune* lauds Kelly for her courage in speaking out (Editorial Board, 2018).

Bates (2017) studied the mental health in 18 women who were targeted by revenge porn. She speculates, based on related research, that revenge porn may be a way for the perpetrator to display power over the subject. The exertion of power has been implicated as a motivation for rape as well. Bates also observes that the strategies for avoiding revenge porn focus on the subject, who is generally a woman, indirectly (and hopefully unintentionally) implying that had they been more judicious about their actions, this would not have happened. The strategies do not focus on the perpetrator.

Bates electronically interviewed 18 female survivors of revenge porn, who ranged in age from 21 to 54 with an average age of 31. All were targeted by a male partner in a heterosexual relationship. Although most had experienced having their photos widely disseminated, a few had the images sent to important people in their lives, and several were blackmailed or threatened that the photos would be released. Bates analyzed her interview data to extract themes of mental health consequences, and coping strategies. In the mental health category, survivors reported losing trust, not just in the perpetrator but in other relationships as well. The betrayal and humiliation by someone they thought cared about them made it difficult to avoid being hyper-cautious in other relationships, particularly with men. Prominent among the survivors were post-traumatic stress disorder, anxiety, and depression. In some cases, suicidal thoughts or a suicide attempt was present. Others were afraid to be in public, due to the public exposure, and others were fearful at night. Many participants reported that their self-esteem and confidence suffered from the experience, and others felt that they had lost control of their lives. One participant noted that she was afraid to go to clubs with friends or be flirtatious, due to a loss of confidence in herself as a sexual person. Several talked about being consumed by questions about the motivation of the perpetrator. Although they recognized the perpetrator was angry about the ended relationship, the degree and intensity of the damage and harm still puzzled them. The stories told by the survivors are harrowing, and the fact that they eventually recovered is a testimony to their resilience.

The coping strategies used by these targets included negative ones: abusing alcohol, ruminating about the experience, and engaging in avoidance and denial of the problem. The positive coping strategies often followed the negative ones, including seeking counseling or therapy and reaching out to help others (one participant became active in an advocacy organization for survivors of revenge porn and another began law school). Most found comfort and safety in the support provided by friends and family who were understanding and present. Others turned to religion for solace, some began writing, and others used humor as a coping mechanism. What is a powerful message in Bates's (2017) study is that the mental health impacts of revenge porn were very similar to those reported by rape survivors, emphasizing the nature and degree of harm caused by this digital aggression.

In addition to psychological consequences, some targets experience harm to their daily lives. For example, Tara Dozier was victimized by revenge porn perpetrated by a former boyfriend (Crowe, 2016). The intimate photos were accompanied by contact information and the name of her employer. As a result, she received horrible threats and messages—and she was dismissed from her job. Annie Seifullah, a New York City school principal, was also punished after an ex-boyfriend circulated intimate photos of her to the superintendent of education and others. He also accused her of various inappropriate sexual liaisons. Although Seifullah was able to show that this was a case of revenge porn, she was at first demoted from principal to teacher, and then, after an administrative trial in 2016, she was suspended for one year without pay and reassigned to a location for "unwanted employees" when she returned. Her offense? Bringing negative attention to the school system, and not protecting the Department of Education (DOE) computer on which her perpetrator loaded the photos (Seifullah, 2018).

THE #METOO MOVEMENT

#MeToo is a national movement to support survivors of sexual violence that was founded by Tarana Burke in 2006. In 2017, after numerous

The #MeToo hashtag has been used roughly 19 million times on Twitter in the past year, and usage often surges around news events

Number of Twitter posts mentioning the #MeToo hashtag, Oct. 15, 2017-Sept. 30, 2018

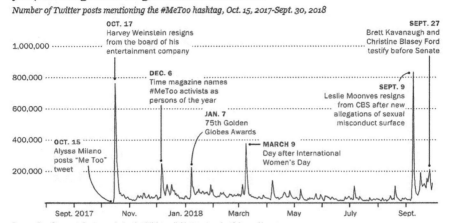

Source: Pew Research Center analysis of publicly available tweets using Crimson Hexagon.

PEW RESEARCH CENTER

Figure 7.1   (The #MeToo hastag has been used roughly 19 million times on Twitter in the past year, and usage often surges around news events. October 11, 2018. Pew Research Center. Available online https://www.pewresearch.org/fact-tank/2018/10/11/how-social-media-users-have-discussed-sexual-harassment-since-metoo-went-viral/ft_18-10-11_metooanniversary_hashtag-used-19m_times/)

allegations about sexual abuse by Harvey Weinstein, a powerful figure in the entertainment industry[3] were made public, the movement was promoted by the viral hashtag #MeToo. In her October 15, 2017, blog, Alyssa Milano, an actress, urged followers to spread the hashtag #MeToo and related her own experience of sexual harassment. The effect was astonishing: The hashtag had been tweeted over half a million times by the next day, and 4.7 million different people (presumably mostly women) used the hashtag in 12 million Facebook posts in the first 24 hours (Lawson, 2018).

The movement has continued to have a large presence online. From October 15, 2017, to September 30, 2018, the hasthag was used on Twitter over 19 million times, with peak uses when there was a related news event (Anderson & Toor, 2018). The single day with the most uses was September 9, 2018, which was when the CEO of CBS resigned in response to reports of sexual misconduct.

Analysis of the tweets revealed that 15% were related to celebrities or the entertainment industry, 14% included personal stories, and 7% mentioned politics in general or specific politicians. Interestingly, when there was news coverage of sexual harassment in 2017, a number of Congresspersons used their Facebook pages to comment on the issue, but female members of both parties were much more likely than males to do so: 61%

of Republican women and 76% of Democratic women compared to 31% of Republican and 46% of Democratic men (Anderson & Toor).

Catherine MacKinnon refers to the #MeToo movement as "the world's first mass movement against sexual abuse" (MacKinnon, 2019, paragraph 1). As noted earlier, this movement quickly attracted many women and has arguably been responsible for more women coming forward to report cases of sexual abuse by powerful men. Sexual harassment laws have made it possible for victims to hold perpetrators accountable, but the #MeToo movement has changed social norms regarding reporting abuse.

In the past, women often chose not to report harassment or abuse because they expected to be dismissed as not credible, accused of inviting the abuse, or having the abuse trivialized. MacKinnon notes that it was up to the woman to prove her allegations, and that the consequences for men were so minimal that it added insult to the injury. The initial sentence (six months in jail) handed down by Judge Arron Persky to Brock Turner for sexual assault of an unconscious woman led to such outrage that the judge was ousted by voters in a recall election (Flynn, 2018). Hayes and Bacon (2018) note that the original sentence was imposed in 2016 prior to the #MeToo movement and that the recall took place after it had built momentum. This was the first recall of a California judge in 86 years!

Judge Persky explained that the light sentence was because a longer sentence would have a "severe impact" on Turner (Baker, 2016, paragraph 1). The victim testified about the impact his behavior had on her. I include excerpts here, this one in relation to the lenient sentence recommended by a probation officer:

> The probation officer weighed the fact that he [Turner] has surrendered a hard earned swimming scholarship. How fast Brock swims does not lessen the severity of what happened to me, and should not lessen the severity of his punishment. If a first time offender from an underprivileged background was accused of three felonies and displayed no accountability for his actions other than drinking, what would his sentence be? The fact that Brock was an athlete at a private university should not be seen as an entitlement to leniency, but as an opportunity to send a message that sexual assault is against the law regardless of social class.

And the following in regard to Turner's refusal to accept responsibility for his actions:

> My life has been on hold for over a year, a year of anger, anguish and uncertainty, until a jury of my peers rendered a judgment that validated the injustices I had endured. Had Brock admitted guilt and remorse and offered to settle early on, I would have considered a lighter sentence, respecting his honesty, grateful to be able to move our lives forward. Instead he took the risk of going to trial, added insult to injury and forced me to relive the hurt as details

about my personal life and sexual assault were brutally dissected before the public. He pushed me and my family through a year of inexplicable, unnecessary suffering, and should face the consequences of challenging his crime, of putting my pain into question, of making us wait so long for justice.

MacKinnon suggests that there were two conditions that made it possible for the #MeToo movement to gain traction. One was the existence of a sexual harassment law. The law (U.S.C. § 1604.11) states: "Harassment on the basis of sex is a violation of section 703 of title VII. 1: Unwelcome sexual advances, requests for sexual favors, and other verbal or physical conduct of a sexual nature constitute sexual harassment" (Code of Federal Regulations, Title 29, Labor). The second was the election of Donald Trump. MacKinnon believes that because of the multiple allegations of sexual abuse against him and the now-infamous recording of his comments regarding the sexual privileges he claimed due to his stardom, many women were outraged, not only that this information was made public, but that it did not make a difference in enough voters to result in his defeat.

I propose that MacKinnon's assessment has merit, but that we must add a third condition: the internet and social media. That is what propelled this movement, and what has given a voice to a group that has historically felt ignored and demeaned by the ways in which sexual assault reports were treated. The hope is that the outpouring of stories and support, and the change in the ways men are treated when credible allegations are made, will change social norms (see Chapter 3) in such a way that dignity and respect are accorded to victims, and censure and consequences are bestowed upon perpetrators.

SUMMARY

In this chapter, I have focused on political issues of importance to women that have been enacted digitally. These topics are likely to be of critical importance in forthcoming elections and beyond. The existence of digital platforms and social media facilitates both egregious behavior—revenge porn and slut-shaming and activism on behalf of women—#MeToo—means that we can anticipate considerable digital interaction about women's issues going forward. I for one hope that disagreements on policy or candidates can be aired respectfully, but it is clear that it is an unlikely scenario. In the next chapter, I will discuss possible ways in which we can reduce or contain digital aggression, the form of cyberbullying this book has described.

Jessica's Story

Cyberaggression may originate and unfold in online spaces, but it can also be that other media provide the fuel for a digital attack. Case in point: JL, a woman in a mid-sized Colorado city whose traumatic experience of domestic violence was reported by the local newspaper. That report spurred a vicious online assault that continues to this day. The attacks on social media were "just as bad as the incident," which is a powerful statement given the story that follows.

JL was dating a man with whom she had been friends for some time, and who was very well known and well liked in the community. He was an avid bodybuilder and used steroids to enhance his muscles. Two weeks prior to the incident, he beat JL and, as a consequence, had an order of protection against him, prohibiting him from seeing her. Nevertheless, on the evening of January 31, he came to her home and beat her badly again. He would not allow her to leave and was threatening to kill her and himself. JL was able to retrieve her phone to call a friend on a pretext and used a coded signal so the friend would know the situation was dangerous and call 911. Once the police arrived, the man barricaded JL and himself in the bedroom where he held her hostage for more than three hours. During that time, he hit her on the head with a propane torch and threatened to blow up the trailer by breaking and igniting the gas line that entered the home in that room. He tried to set fire to JL and burned some clothing before extinguishing the fire at police request. Ultimately, the SWAT team entered the room because JL screamed that he was about to carry out his threat to blow up the trailer home. He did not obey police commands and was shot and killed by a deputy. JL was transported to the hospital by ambulance to be treated for "serious bodily injury including multiple facial fractures."

The incident occurred on January 31, and first news report seems to have been a radio news item. That report cited the local newspaper as the source of its information and noted that the man had been killed and that the woman was not injured. The newspaper also reported again on February 4 that law enforcement had reported that she was not seriously hurt. That report noted that JL had declined to comment for their article.

JL recalls that the newspaper request was not simply for a comment, but for a video interview. Given her condition, it is not surprising that she declined. Furthermore, her traumatic experience—being badly beaten, threatened with death, held hostage, witnessing the deadly shooting of her boyfriend by police—was so recent that she was simply not ready. She provided names of friends they might talk to, but those persons were not contacted.

Instead, the February 4 article in the local newspaper included comments from friends of the man, who blamed JL for the man's behavior. They indicated that he had been happy and normal until he began this relationship, when he "spiraled out of control." Another interviewee referred to his "toxic relationship" with JL as the cause of his changed behavior. One hinted at possible substance abuse. According to JL, the man had recently obtained his steroids from a new overseas source, and she believes that perhaps that accounted for the behavioral changes that she noticed as well. Many of the side effects of steroids were present in the man: aggressive behavior, paranoia, delusions, mood swings. Nevertheless, the story included inaccurate information (that she was not injured) and quoted persons who were angry and bitter, and who blamed JL for the death. These quotes provided fuel for the storm of attacks on social media that continue to appear. They often are not on JL's wall, but if she comments on someone's post on Facebook, others will use the opportunity to malign and demean her. Others have unfriended her because they "don't want her posts on their wall," implying she is a pariah to be avoided.

Although JL has suffered other harassment and serious mistreatment offline because of this incident, the ongoing and public shaming she experienced online has been the most detrimental. The supportive comments are there too but are diminished by the vitriolic and hurtful nastiness that has caused her deep psychological wounds.

Because this case of cyberbullying is linked to the traditional media, I interviewed a television news anchor/investigative reporter. Traditional news media have been called "fake news" and soundly criticized for inaccuracies in their reporting. Different news sources—print and digital— have varying degrees of bias, so that their editorials, newscasts, and so on often espouse or support a consistent political viewpoint. Some see this as biased reporting; others see it as a way to find sources with which they align. Local television news is not immune to the criticism that has been leveled at national platforms, but they serve a different purpose and different audience.

The journalist is a native of the city where she works. Given that the station is local, it is the local stories that arouse the ire of a subset of the audience, and that can lead to cyberaggression. Although comments are often critical of protagonists in the story, the newscaster/reporters are attacked as well. Those attacks may come in the form of comments on the digital story, posts on Facebook, tweets, and e-mails. There are also phone complaints, which this journalist finds easier to respond to and defuse because there is real-time interaction. When viewers are unhappy with a story (usually because they have a personal connection or investment in the subject) they may demean the anchor's appearance, disparage her clothes or hairdo, rather than offering rational critiques about the content. At times, she has been accused of telling lies because the local audience was shocked at what she reported or because viewers felt loyal to the individuals or entities covered in the story. Although this journalist has not been directly threatened, nor have her personal details been publicized, she has received vague comments such as "You'll pay for this." Although she denies feeling frightened (personal note: that comment would scare me!), she is also cautious; she is intentional about where she parks her vehicle and has learned maneuvers to detect if she is being followed.

This experienced journalist agrees that social norms have become unclear in our society, providing a platform for angry voices and vicious attacks that no longer are always sanctioned. She suggested that people (often of the millennial generation) first test the waters, making a remark online that is in questionable taste. When that does not result in disapproval, and/or garners support, the person is emboldened to do this more often. She perceives a kind of mob mentality online, with critical and rude commentary widely observed and thus normalized. She believes that on social media and online news sites, visitors tend to skim headlines rather than read entire stories, and then form opinions based on the limited information a headline provides. Although she acknowledges that the easy availability of social media and blog platforms contributes to this hostile climate, she also believes there are generational differences in the consumption of news that are important. For example, older generations tend to still look to broadcast news as a primary source of current events, while millennials and younger persons tend to rely more on digital sources.

When the journalist investigated and reported on allegations of bullying of a student by a school employee, the initial reaction of many viewers was to discount the report, and to criticize the reporter for daring to suggest that this prominent person could behave in such a way. This is the kind of local news that engages the local audience and generates strong reactions, which are often expressed online. When the investigation was complete, and the allegations upheld, the tone changed, and the anger and rude comments were directed at the individual.

This journalist was emphatic about the ethical code that governs her profession and insists that journalists have an obligation to be neutral reporters of facts. But the fact that bloggers and talk show hosts do not have the same standards has contributed to the deterioration of the online environment.

NOTES

1. See Belluck (2019) at https://www.nytimes.com/2019/05/09/health/state-abortion-laws.html for a brief discussion of the medical opinions on this question.

2. It occurred pre social media but not pre-Internet. In fact, the Drudge Report (see later in the chapter) was an early blog that collected and published online high-interest news items.

3. The public revelations about Weinstein's behavior first appeared in an October 5, 2017, article in the *New York Times* by Kantor and Twohey.

8

Managing Digital Aggression

The disturbing phenomenon of digital aggression/cyberbullying is unlikely to disappear, and the platforms used for such purposes are sure to proliferate over time. We know cyberbullying is not a problem only for children and adolescents, and the political arena, broadly defined, seems to be fertile ground for various forms of digital aggression. Rather than plunge into helplessness, however, in this chapter I consider how digital aggression can be managed to reduce the harm it causes.

GLOBAL STRATEGIES

Because the Internet is global in both access and scope, global actions may be necessary to rein in digital aggressors, especially those with more harmful intent than simply "going for the lulz." In March 2019, 51 Muslim worshippers were slaughtered by an assailant in Christchurch, New Zealand. The attack was livestreamed (e.g., broadcast in real time, as it occurred) over Facebook's social network. There is good evidence (e.g., Pfefferbaum et al., 2014) that viewing media coverage of disasters (including acts of terrorism) is associated with post-traumatic stress disorder, post-traumatic stress, depression, anxiety, and so on. It is logical to think that watching a real-time act as horrific as that in Christchurch would have serious psychological consequences around the world and that the use of social media as part of this heinous act constitutes digital aggression/cyberbullying on a mass scale.

On May 14, 2019, Facebook announced that it will restrict livestreaming so that those who misuse the service will be barred from the platform for 30 days, on the first offense. The Christchurch attacker had also posted a manifesto about the planned attack on 8chan, but it was written with extremist jargon and ironic references that obscured the intent to all but the most dedicated insiders. Jacinda Ardern, prime minister of New Zealand, said that it is important to address the "coded" language that makes it difficult to detect extremist plots. Even though Facebook was alerted and removed the video promptly, others who had made copies were able to continue to circulate it on YouTube, Twitter, and Instagram (Lorenz, 2019). The first report about the video was not made until 29 minutes after it began (Elliott, 2019).

Facebook's new livestreaming strategy is clearly a step in the right direction, but some have called for more severe penalties, such as fines or jail time for platforms that do not promptly remove violent and extremist content. An international dialogue known as the Christchurch Call was held in Paris in May 2019, at which discussions among 18 governments and 5 major U.S. tech firms focused on the need to address such horrific acts at the international level (Metz & Satariano, 2019). Government representatives along with executives from the major social media platforms gathered to consider what strategies, both technical and legislative, could be implemented to address the challenge. Participants pledged to work together, acknowledging that the varied interest of tech companies and governments won't be easy to reconcile.

THE UNITED STATES

It is discouraging that the American government declined to sign the nonbinding pledge along with other world leaders and social media companies to increase efforts to constrain use of social media by those whose intention is to promote violence and spread hate online. Critics noted that the absence of the United States as a signatory was a serious matter. The reason given for opting not to join the other nations was concern about free speech, which is a theme that underlies most of the forms of digital aggression discussed in this book. That is, the absence of any restrictions on online content is hailed by some as a welcome freedom, and there is strong resistance to regulating that environment, even when consequences are so damaging.

The relevant words are: "Congress shall make no law . . . abridging the freedom of speech." This does not mean, however, that the right to free speech is absolute.

The First Amendment of the U.S. Constitution was briefly reviewed in Chapter 1, but it bears additional scrutiny now. The relevant words are: "Congress shall make no law . . . abridging the freedom of speech." This does not mean, however, that the right to free speech is absolute. Supreme Court rulings have determined that the First Amendment does *not* permit someone to do the following:

- To incite actions that would harm others (e.g., "[S]hout[ing] 'fire' in a crowded theater.")—*Schenck v. United States*, 249 U.S. 47 (1919).

- To make or distribute obscene materials—*Roth v. United States*, 354 U.S. 476 (1957).

- To burn draft cards as an antiwar protest—*United States v. O'Brien*, 391 U.S. 367 (1968).

- To permit students to print articles in a school newspaper over the objections of the school administration—*Hazelwood School District v. Kuhlmeier*, 484 U.S. 260 (1988).

- Of students to make an obscene speech at a school-sponsored event—*Bethel School District #43 v. Fraser*, 478 U.S. 675 (1986).

- Of students to advocate illegal drug use at a school-sponsored event—*Morse v. Frederick*, __ U.S. __ (2007). (g). (United States Courts, n.d., https://www.uscourts.gov/about-federal-courts/educational-resour ces/about-educational-outreach/activity-resources/what-does, screen 1)

There are a few landmark cases that established limits on freedom of speech, and I will summarize them here. The First Amendment to the U.S. Constitution was adopted in 1791, after being ratified by 10 (out of 14) states. Only seven years later, when Congress anticipated a war with France, Congress passed the Sedition Act, which limited free speech. This act made it illegal to publicly oppose the government, and imposed fines and/or imprisonment on anyone who would "write, print, utter, or publish . . . any false, scandalous and malicious writing" against the government (ushistory.org., n.d.). There was strong opposition to the law, and the state of Virginia threatened to secede because of it. Although the law conflicted with the First Amendment, it was not reviewed by the Supreme Court, and was allowed to expire in 1801.

A landmark case for the Supreme Court was its ruling in *Schenck v. US*, 249 U.S. 47 (1919). Congress passed the Federal Espionage Act in 1917, during World War I. This law made it illegal to make false statements that would interfere with military forces or aid the enemy. Penalties were harsh, including large fines and long prison sentences. The next year, an additional law, the Sedition Act of 1918, prohibited statements that included "disloyal, profane, scurrilous, or abusive language" toward the

Constitution, the government, the military uniform, or the flag. More than 2,100 people were prosecuted, including Charles Schenck, who sent 15,000 leaflets through the mail in which he encouraged men who were drafted to not "submit to intimidation" and to "petition for repeal" of the draft law that had been passed in 1917. The Supreme Court rendered a unanimous decision that affirmed the constitutionality of restricting free speech that violated the Espionage Act. The ruling proclaimed that speech that creates a "clear and present danger" can be prohibited. In his decision, Oliver Wendell Holmes said that the leaflets in question, which urged people to resist the military draft during World War I, were tantamount to "shouting 'Fire!' in a crowded theater," which is not protected speech. Some of Holmes's words in that decision are notable:

> "When a nation is at war, many things that might be said in a time of peace are such a hindrance to its effort that their utterance will not be endured so long as men fight, and that no Court could regard them as protected by any constitutional right." and
>
> The most stringent protection of free speech would not protect a man in falsely shouting fire in a theatre and causing a panic. . . . The question in every case is whether the words are used in such circumstances and are of such a nature as to create a clear and present danger that they will bring about the substantive evils that Congress has a right to prevent. (Waimberg, 2015)

A restriction on free speech was also allowed in the case of *Chaplinsky v. New Hampshire*, 315 U.S. 568 (1942). Chaplinsky had been convicted of violating a state law that "prohibited intentionally offensive, derisive, or annoying speech to any person who is lawfully in a street or public area." Chaplinsky had been distributing Jehovah's Witness literature on a public sidewalk and had used derogatory terms about the town marshal. He appealed the conviction saying that the state law violated the First Amendment. The court disagreed and unanimously upheld his conviction:

> There are certain well-defined and narrowly limited classes of speech, the prevention and punishment of which have never been thought to raise any constitutional problem. These include the lewd and obscene, the profane, the libelous, and the insulting or "fighting" words those which by their very utterance inflict injury or tend to incite an immediate breach of the peace. It has been well observed that such utterances are no essential part of any exposition of ideas, and are of such slight social value as a step to truth that any benefit that may be derived from them is clearly outweighed by the social interest in order and morality. (Supreme Court justice Frank Murphy, in the unanimous decision on the case)

On the other hand, in *Cohen v. California* (403 U.S. 15, 1971) the court found that "certain offensive words and phrases" to convey political messages cannot be prohibited, even those that might offend others. Cohen, a 19-year-old who was against the U.S. involvement in the Vietnam War, was in a courthouse (for a legitimate purpose) wearing a jacket that had "Fuck the Draft" on it. Although an officer noticed this and asked the judge to hold Cohen in contempt of court, the judge refused to do so. He was, however, the arrested and convicted for "disturbing the peace," and sentenced to 30 days in jail.

Cohen appealed the decision, and the Supreme Court ultimately ruled (on a 5–4 vote) that Cohen's freedom of speech could not be abridged simply because it was offensive, and importantly, that even heightened emotional, and perhaps vulgar words, did not constitute "fighting words." Such language is the result of the free exchange of ideas, which is protected by the First Amendment. In that ruling, Justice Harlan stated:

> For the First and Fourteenth Amendments have never been thought to give absolute protection to every individual to speak whenever or wherever he pleases, or to use any form of address in any circumstances that he chooses. (Legal Information Institute, n.d.)

Interestingly, the dissent argued that wearing the jacket was not speech but an action, which could be restricted. A brief and useful video about the case can be viewed at https://www.youtube.com/watch?v=SfzliHhO6lY.

The final case I will mention is that of Arthur Terminiello (*Terminiello v. Chicago*, 337 US1, 1949). The incident occurred not long after World War II, and Terminiello gave a speech in Chicago to a large audience in which he said that Hitler was correct and that Democrats, Jews, and communists were destroying the country (www.crfa-usa.org, n.d.). There were protesters outside the auditorium, and although there were police present, the crowd was agitated and several disturbances occurred (Legal Information Institute, n.d.). Terminiello was found guilty of disorderly conduct, and the case made its way to the Supreme Court. In his majority opinion overturning the conviction, Justice Douglas made several important points that express the necessity of a strict interpretation of the First Amendment:

> Accordingly a function of free speech under our system of government is to invite dispute. It may indeed best serve its high purpose when it induces a condition of unrest, creates dissatisfaction with conditions as they are, or even stirs people to anger. Speech is often provocative and challenging. It may strike at prejudices and preconceptions and have profound unsettling effects as it presses for acceptance of an idea. That is why freedom of speech, though not absolute, . . . is nevertheless protected against censorship or punishment, unless shown likely to produce a *clear and present danger of a serious substantive evil* [italics added for emphasis] that rises far above public inconvenience, annoyance, or unrest. . . . There is no room under our

Constitution for a more restrictive view. For the alternative would lead to standardization of ideas either by legislatures, courts, or dominant political or community groups.

The fundamental issue of free speech recently emerged from readers in the comments responding to Warzel's (2019a) OpEd about the responsibilities of social media companies for the livestreaming of the New Zealand massacre of Muslims, discussed in more detail later. This excerpt is from a comment by chickenlover:

> Even though we all agree that there should be free speech, I think most of us will also agree that there are limits to free speech. The most often quoted example is that we cannot yell "Fire" in a public place just because we have the ability to do so. And that is exactly the point. Just because one has the ability to upload content, be it pictures, videos, or words, one does/should not have the right to upload content that incites and creates mass hysteria.

Another commenter, Stevelo, reiterates the thorny issues around limiting free speech, saying, in part, "Freedom of speech is primarily designed to prevent censorship of unpopular speech. What you see as propaganda, others see as speaking the truth." And MikeG weighs in as well:

> It's time to think about the First Amendment and whether we need to constrain the use of global/widely-consumed media to licensed individuals. We already prohibit yelling "fire" in a crowded theater, or in cases of slander/libel, or conspiracy to commit crime. So we have reasonable constraints that have in no way jeopardized the free speech that we cherish. At the same time, we place constraints on activities that could cause serious harm to people, animals, or property by licensing everything from vehicle operation to medical practice to law to you-name-it.

These cases suggest that the court has recognized that the right to free speech is broad but is not absolute, and that under certain situations and contexts, restrictions can be imposed. I am not a legal scholar, so I cannot presume to speculate whether some of the extreme forms of digital aggression we have seen constitute a clear and present danger of a serious substantive evil. Although we know that other laws (e.g., harassment) may apply to a given case, it seems that extremist content that threatens the safety of the public might reasonably be banned. I realize this is not even on the radar of our legislatures, but I hope that we at some point will engage in discussions with other democracies that have taken measures to preserve the many benefits of digital technology without endangering the lives or jobs or reputations of member of our communities.

Realistically, I don't hold any hope that meaningful legislation will be proposed or passed anytime soon, so perhaps we should turn to what social media platforms and other providers of digital access might do. However, we must consider the scope of the task to entertain practical ideas. Warzel (2019b) offers data that provide some perspective. The video of the New Zealand attack saw 1.5 million upload attempts in the first 24 hours, although Facebook's detection system blocked 1.2 million of those. The remaining 300,000 copies remained on the platform and thus could be seen and shared or liked, by the two billion subscribers to that social media site. YouTube also saw multiple efforts to disseminate the video, which was uploaded immediately following the incident as often as one per second. Warzel appreciates the numbers provided by these two sites but is skeptical of their intention. He believes that the data are insufficient. For example, Facebook did not reveal how many views and other actions were taken on the 300,000 copies of the attack before they were deleted. He opines that the tech companies were trying to present themselves as aware and actively working to thwart those who would use the sites to purvey terror, and perhaps more importantly, that they focused on moderation of content rather than their role in enabling online extremism that leads to offline disasters such as this one.

It is noteworthy that Australia has a new law—the Sharing of Abhorrent Violent Material bill—that impose fines and punishment for social media sites that do not remove hate content (whether it is posted within Australia or elsewhere) expeditiously and the material reported to police. The bill has its share of critics (e.g., there is no definition of expeditious), and it will be interesting to see whether revisions will be made. The United Kingdom is considering making social media executives personally responsible for damaging content that is disseminated on their platforms (Gunia, 2019). They outlined their views in a recent white paper, but it appears there will be further discussions and revisions before the ideas are proposed as legislation.

Bates (2017) is concerned with the harmful mental health consequences of victims of revenge porn, and she notes that many states have laws against nonconsensual pornography, and that revenge porn can sometimes be prosecuted under those laws. However, she notes that the classification of the crime, and the associated penalties, varies widely from state to state, and recommends that legislatures craft laws making revenge porn a sexual offense. A law called the Intimate Privacy Protection Act was introduced in the House of Representatives in 2016, and was referred to committee and then a subcommittee, but at the time of this writing, no further action was taken. The law reads:

> To amend title 18, United States Code, to provide that it is unlawful to knowingly distribute a private, visual depiction of a person's intimate parts or of a person engaging in sexually explicit conduct, with reckless disregard for the person's lack of consent to the distribution, and for other purposes.

While new laws might make a statement that these actions are unacceptable, they do not often serve as deterrents. It also puts the burden on the victim to produce evidence and make complaints and so on, which may feel as though they are being re-victimized.

TECH COMPANIES

At the Christchurch Call meeting in Paris, tech companies proposed to implement a nine-point menu of technical strategies, including improving and adding to existing user systems for reporting inappropriate content, improving automatic systems for detecting problematic posts, improved review of live-streaming content, and collaborative development of research programs. Since the real-time broadcast of the Christchurch attacks was a stimulus for the meeting, Facebook announced a new policy that would ban a person who violates its rules (including livestreaming terrorist material) on the first offense.

Warzel (2019a) believes that these social media platforms encourage the posting of extremist content because it brings attention (viewers, likes, shares, etc.), which may also then attract advertisers, the bread-and-butter of the sites. There is a new feature—SuperChat—on YouTube that accepts donations to the performer during a livestream. Warzel believes that this feature is functioning as "online telethons for white nationalists."

We should consider that extremist actions can invite digital aggression from those online bullies who seize the news to spread their anger. In October 2018, 11 Jews were killed in their synagogue in Pittsburgh, Pennsylvania. Simon and Sidner (2019) analyzed Google searches for "Jews must die," "Kill Jews," and "I hate Jews," following that incident, and after another in April 2019 in Poway, California. Their graph shows prominent spikes in the number of searches for those phrases following both incidents. These journalists interviewed a Jewish woman who remarked that the searches feel like personal attacks to her. Hopefully, she did not see the posts on 8chan's /pol/board that said the Poway shooter that he was "a f***** underachiever," because there was only one death. There were also many comments that encouraged viewers to "kill them all." Simon and Sidner noted that the most common kinds of posts were those that said that both attacks were perpetrated by Jews in order to gain sympathy and to cover up their illegal activities. Other posts praised the killers and their manifestos. These are acts of digital aggression, causing psychological trauma in those who see them.

At the Christchurch Call, the tech companies (Amazon, Facebook, Google, Microsoft, and Twitter) pledged to increase information sharing with governments (Romm & Harwell, 2019). Other experts have recommended a time-delay for livestreaming. A delay, according to some, would have allowed Facebook and other social media to remove the video before it was broadcast. The only practical way to do this, says Warzel (2019b), is to determine whether to do this with all livestreaming, or only from certain accounts. The technical systems for identifying violent content would likely identify false positives, which would be problematic. Human moderators might do better, but they cost more than artificial intelligence and are less accurate. And the scale is monumental. YouTube content is uploaded at a rate of more than 400 videos per minute, and in 2015, Facebook divulged that its videos received eight billion views per day. These are staggering numbers, making the moderation task, were it to be extended, daunting to say the least. As is the case with several of these recommendations, clear and specific guidelines would need to be developed so that the moderators had guidelines to follow.

Warzel (2019a, b) discusses tech companies' roles and reminds us that all social media sites have terms of use agreements to which subscribers must agree. So there is a mechanism in place to ban users who violate those rules. Wanzel reports that Twitter suspended 1.2 million accounts of terrorists since 2015, which is to say that the system is working to an extent. The Christchurch event highlighted a thorny issue, however, which is that journalists may have also shared or reposted the video in their perceived role to keep the public informed. Wanzel hopes that tech companies will now be more willing to make clear policies prohibiting any post or sharing of terrorist content or mass violence.

Wanzel goes on to comment that New Zealand immediately banned viewing, possessing, or distributing the Christchurch video. Australian tech companies blocked access to sites that continued to host the video (8chan, 4chan, Voat, and Liveleak). Although nothing close to such actions has been instituted in the United States, he hopes that other countries' actions will be an impetus for important discussions of how to define a violent or terrorist act (versus news reports of the act) in a way that is consistent with the First Amendment protections. In the meantime, it appears there may be some increase in moderation of the sites by the companies themselves. One example Wanzel provides is that after the Pittsburgh synagogue shooting, a hosting provider, Joyent, suspended service for a social network (Gab) that contained posts by the shooting subject that were anti-Semitic and hinted at conspiracy to commit the shooting. He also reports that the poster whose threat of ethnic cleansing in Charlottesville, Virginia, closed local schools for several days was arrested after an intense investigation by police and FBI. This strategy of getting assistance from law enforcement is one he hopes to see more often.

8chan and 4chan have no interest in curbing the toxic content that is the appeal of the forums. Warzel (2019b) points out that these sites, although much smaller than the major sites typically mentioned, are often where offensive memes and content are created and tested, and then spread on larger, better subscribed social media. However, if the sites are unwilling to limit content in any way, internet service providers (ISPs) could block access, although whether they would take such a drastic step is unknown.

A provocative view of the role of social media platforms is relevant for this discussion. DeNardis and Hackl (2015) discuss governance of social media, arguing that the absence of governmental regulation of the content posted on those sites (see Section 230 of the Communications Decency Act (CDA), 1996, which the authors note is "one of the most important guarantors of free expression on the internet"), the sites themselves become de facto arbiters of the rights and rules for their use. They further assert that "individual expression as a core purpose of their services," referring to private social media companies. Social media companies are often located in the United States, but their subscribers are global, making it challenging to develop laws that would apply to all countries where subscribers are located. Thus, the companies must self-regulate to keep users safe (Grygiel & Brown, 2019).

DeNardis and Hackl (2015) note that most social media sites allow the user to determine how much information is public and what is private. But they also require users to provide real names and other demographic information in order to obtain an account. They are critical of this practice, saying that Facebook's practice both limits one's ability for creative expression of one's identity and endangers the safety of certain marginalized groups, who can be targeted for cyberbullying and harassment on and offline if their group membership is obvious. They also oppose the broad collection of metadata by social media sites, which are used to profile users for targeted advertising. The metadata are shared with third-party advertisers who use them for their own business activities. "Social media platforms are largely free services that monetize customer data as their core online advertising revenue model" (DeNardis & Hackl, 2015, p. 9). Another concern raised by these scholars is that social media sites sometimes disclose this personal information to governments, in response to requests the site determines are legitimate situations in which the privacy of the data is less important than the reason for obtaining it.

Given that there are no legal requirements for social media companies to moderate content, and the CDA limits their liability for content posted by third parties, Grygiel and Brown (2019) consider whether the companies might have incentives to do content moderation on their initiative. These scholars are concerned with revenge porn in particular (see Chapter 7) and terrorism, and also consider the additional burdens for monitoring that accompany new technologies such as livestreaming. They appeal to corporate social responsibility, and hope that the business advantages of having a reputation as a socially responsible company would serve as motivators.

Social media have terms of service to which subscribers agree, which allows them to remove content that is inconsistent with those policies. Social media websites moderate content by using a combination of coding algorithms, user reports of infractions, and human review. Content moderation can be accomplished by placing warning labels on some content, which must first be identified by users and verified by the company. They can also provide tools for users to block subscribers or content so they do not have to see it. However, Gyrgiel and Brown (2019) point out that there are no uniform standards for how long the sites can take to remove content such as revenge porn. Because of the large volume of content on the sites, moderation schemes must contend with hate speech, cyberbullying via racism or homophobic slurs, harassment, and violence. They point to steps in the right direction taken by Facebook, for example, which banned revenge porn in 2015 along with other sexually violent material and has added a new tool in 2017 in a further attempt to identify and remove revenge porn.

Grygiel and Brown (2019) make what seem to me to be reasonable suggestions for protecting users of social media. First, they suggest that government-supported task forces might encourage social media sites to be more consistent, but it is not likely to have a major impact. Their major recommendations for social media in the short term are to provide feedback to reporters of problematic content so they know whether the content has been reviewed and what action was taken (or not). Public reports of moderation data would also provide a level of transparency on the part of the sites, which would be helpful. They also strongly recommend drastically increasing the size of human moderators, given the volume of material to review. They also propose that to better monitor such problems as revenge porn, companies should also invest in the development of new technology to identify such content. Finally, they recommend the formation of an industry self-regulation body, which exists in many industries, that would support such measures as ensuring all social media sites have easily visible and usable reporting mechanisms.

A survey conducted in August 2017 found that 59% of their representative sample of U.S. adults believed the social media platforms were not doing enough to suppress cyberbullying (Nguyen, 2017). The question of whether government is doing enough was not asked in that survey, but the answer would be interesting.

OTHER MEDIA

We noted earlier in the book that traditional media (television news, print news, and radio) look to social media for breaking news, since online sources can post news as soon as it breaks, and traditional outlets must wait until the next edition or broadcast to do so. One of the ways traditional media could reduce the harm from digital aggression is to cease amplifying bullying behaviors. Sullivan (2019) bemoans the frequency of the nicknames Trump has created and repeated about other politicians— think Crooked Hillary, Pocahontas, Lyin' Ted, and the Failing *New York Times*. She believes the more Trump is threatened by an opponent, the nastier the nickname. Joe Biden is a serious contender and has been dubbed SleepyCreepyJoe. Sullivan believes these epithets are intended to bully, and that the media are complicit by repeating their use. Sullivan offers recommendations for media, both traditional and online: Never use the nicknames in a headline, in a tweet, in the running text on the bottom of a screen, or in a news alert. She contends that those are the places that do the most harm.

POLITICIANS

It is clear that politicians must use social media to connect with voters and with their constituents. Social media provides immediate, unfiltered access to the public. This is such an important component of their activities that most have staff members dedicated to navigating social media sites. Trump is known for personally communicating his thoughts, and often policy or personnel decisions, directly via Twitter. His tweets are seen not only by his followers on Twitter but by the general public via shares and retweets as well as reporting in other media. We have noted that Trump's tweets freely use pejorative nicknames and insults that are examples of cyberbullying: They are intended to harm others, they are repeated (either by him or others), and he has more power than his targets. YouGov Plc sampled 1,100 U.S. adults and used weights so that their findings are representative of all U.S. adults (Nguyen, 2017). Results revealed that 61% of Americans agreed or strongly agreed with the statement, "President Trump acts like a cyberbully on social media," while only 27% disagreed. Respondents who identified as Black had a 78% rate of agreement on that item, higher than other race/ethnic groups. Not surprisingly, 89% of Democrats agreed, as did 36% of Republicans. Forty-one percent agreed that "President Trump's use of social media allows him to better connect with young people," including 50% of male respondents and 33% of females. Further, 50% of participants indicated that the amount of cyberbullying had increased over the last year.

Although not a politician, Melania Trump has status as the First Lady, and she made a campaign promise to stop cyberbullying, naming her initiative "Be Best." In the survey cited above, 35% said they were aware of her pledge, but 60% said they were not aware of any of her efforts post-election.

She has been subjected to harsh criticism of this pledge given that her husband is the cyberbully in chief (Miller, 2018). She says she is aware of the criticism but not deterred from her goal of helping children (Gajanan, 2018). It is not clear that she acknowledges the extent of cyberbullying—and the damage that it causes—among adults.

The 2016 election campaign generated a lot of interest in how politicians used social media. Pew Research Center found that 25% of those on social media follow politicians, 65% of whom follow those whose views align with their own. Quorum (2018) reported on Twitter, Facebook, and Instagram posts on their official accounts by members of the 115th Congress from January through November 2018. Ninety-five percent of senators and 97% of members of the House posted on Facebook, 100% of Senate and 99% of House members used Twitter, YouTube was used by 93% of senators and 84% of members of the House, and 70% of senators and 50% of representatives posted on Instagram. In that period of time, the most used hashtag was #taxreform, the most active tweeter in the Senate was Senator Marco Rubio, while Senator Bernie Sanders was the leader on Facebook. On Instagram, the most posts were made by Senator Chuck Grassley, and Senator Heitkamp used YouTube the most. In the House of Representatives, Representative Maloney was the leader on Twitter, while Representative Khanna was the most prolific poster on Facebook, Representative O'Rourke was dominant on Instagram, and the YouTuber in first place was Representative Carter. To get a sense of the subjects of the members of Congress, Quorum tallied the top hashtags used overall: #taxreform, #sotu (state of the union), #taxcutsandjobsact, #goptaxscam, and #scotus. These varied by party, with top Republican hashtags as follows: #taxreform, #taxcutsandjobsact, #betteroffnow, while for Democrats, the top three were #netneutrality, #goptaxscam, and #sotu.

On Facebook, users can indicate their reaction to posts by clicking on buttons, which expanded from an initial "like" option to include angry, love, sad, haha, and wow. Between February 24, 2016, and Election Day 2016, legislators' posts garnered 3.6 million "angry" reactions, but in the same span of time after the election, angry reactions were used 14 million times. In contrast, love was used 7 million times in the earlier period and 12 million after. Those Facebook posts that opposed other politicians or parties (15% of all the posts were of this type) were more likely to receive angry reactions.

In the 115th Congress, Hughes and Lam (2017) found that the most liberal and conservative members had much greater numbers of followers than did moderates. I think it's safe to speculate that social media users who are interested in politics seek information from politicians who share their worldviews. It is likely that staff members and

Confrontational congressional posts most likely to receive angry reactions

% of all reactions to Facebook posts by members of Congress that were ...

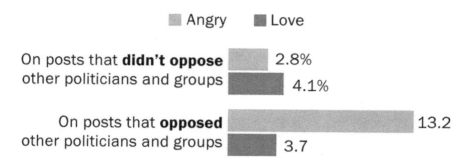

Source: Pew Research Center analysis of Facebook posts created by members of Congress between Feb. 24, 2016 and Dec. 31, 2017.

PEW RESEARCH CENTER

Figure 8.1   Hughes, A., & Van Kessel, P. (2018, July 18). *"Anger" topped "love" when Facebook users reacted to lawmakers' posts after 2016 election.* Washington, DC: Pew Research Center. Available online https://www.pewresearch.org/fact-tank/2018/07/18/anger-topped-love-facebook-after-2016-election/)

congresspersons don't actually read the comments and reactions of viewers, but they do count them, to get a sense of how much interest there is in a particular topic.

I close this section with an e-mail message I received from a politician. I had contacted a number of politicians seeking to learn about their experiences with cyberbullying. I assumed that as political public figures, they would be subjected to lots of attacks. Several state legislators who were kind enough to speak with me said their social media accounts are handled by staffers, so they don't view the comments and responses very often. They also have been instructed that any message they receive that even hints of violence or threats should be immediately reported to the police.

What struck me about the e-mail from Mitzi Epstein of the Arizona House of Representatives is her ability to see what underlies many angry posts and respond appropriately. It would be a huge step forward if more politicians were able to do this.

> Politicians have to be able to take criticism. Democracy must work that way. Without criticisms, elected officials would be tyrants. I hold myself to a higher standard than other folks. Elected officials need a thicker skin than others.
>
> When people communicate to those who are not politicians, I believe that common decency requires polite words, and any steps away from courtesy may be bullying. Bullying is usually wrong. It produces harmful results and makes most situations worse. When people bully others, their bullying should be ignored or purposefully stopped, imho.
>
> However, when people communicate with me as their representative, I am willing to put up with some vitriol. When people give me harsh criticisms as their representative, I try to get to the problem they are trying to express. I give them a lot of leeway to make harsh statements because under their bad language, name-calling, and stereotyping is an expression of a valid fear, concern, or problem. It is my job to listen to them. Sometimes, after they realize I am listening to them the hatred and name-calling stop. Not always.
>
> That is my way of explaining that in my view people do not bully me. They express their fears using communication skills that are not polite and not kind sometimes, but I do my best to actually listen when it's valid and shrug it off when it's not. So I cannot remember any examples of bullying. We need better systems for people to learn how to express their valid fears and concerns without attacking and scapegoating others. We as a species need better communication skills. (M. Epstein, personal communication, February 23, 2019)

INDIVIDUALS

What can individuals do to stem the tide of cyberbullying and digital aggression, especially in the current partisan political context? Although these suggestions may appear simplistic, we know that small changes add up and might make a difference.

1. Don't feed the trolls. That is, don't respond at all when someone is obviously seeking a reaction. Their goal is to get you angry, so do not cooperate.

2. When looking for information on the internet or social media

> Don't feed the trolls. That is, don't respond at all when someone is obviously seeking a reaction. Their goal is to get you angry, so do not cooperate.

sites to join, take the time to research the sites. Unsuspecting people can be lured to sites like 8chan by following a link and experience shock and dismay when reading some of the content.

3.   It is probably obvious, but nevertheless important, to be familiar with the affordances of sites you use. Take the time to set appropriate privacy settings, to learn how to report offensive content, to learn where to seek help if a site doesn't respond to requests to remove offensive content or revenge porn.

4.   Recognize that some people enjoy argument or debate, almost as sport. Learning how to express one's point of view, or to disagree with someone else's, without resorting to ad hominem attacks or red herrings will enhance your ability to have your position heard. In the same vein, there are urban "contests" (think the Dozens, or ranking) for creative insults. In these games, the contestants take turns insulting each other, with the goal to create an insult so outrageous that a worse one is impossible. Such activity is often more sporting than intentionally harmful—but when one doesn't recognize that the game is on, it's easy to be wounded.

5.   Take advice from the stories of Nolan Cabrera and Michelle Pitot. They have strong views and passionate convictions about issues that are not universally applauded. They expect that there will be negative comments to their online posts, and believe that in order to be accountable, they must read posts, and when there's an opportunity to correct an error or point out flaws in argument, they do so. They do not respond to comments that are simply nasty.

6.   When bombarded with attacks, follow the example of Liam Hackett. Recall that he had a friend read the comments and was alerted only if a comment was a threat so he could notify authorities.

It is my fervent hope that readers are better equipped to understand and manage political cyberbullying and digital aggression. The rapid expansion of social media and other interactive technology underlines the importance of this topic. Further, as future elections elevate political tempers, we must be judicious in how we engage with technology. Leading up to the 2016 presidential election, 37% of social media users said they were "worn out" by the barrage of political material, compared to 20% who enjoyed seeing and engaging with political material. Furthermore, 59% who found themselves in discussions or debates with someone with whom they disagreed said those interactions were "stressful and frustrating," while 35% found them worthwhile. I know that when I find someone's posts consistently offensive, I simply block them so I am not faced with them when I log on to my social media. By choosing my online news sources carefully, I typically am able to find both news and OpEds that are accurate and well argued, even though some will take positions I oppose. These strategies work for me, and I hope readers will develop strategies to keep themselves safe and sane as the world continues to play out in the digital universe.

I end with some quotes from a news story about yet another case of cyberbullying (Blake, 2109). Describing the intensity of the threats and horrible epithets used against a target of cyberbullying, Blake said, "What would inspire someone to talk to a stranger in that way? It's because rage has become the fuel of online discourse." And, reflecting on another case in which a person, wrongly accused of racism on Facebook, was the target of a barrage of cyberbullying on the site, he observed, "But truth is unimportant in online shame culture, Kain [another writer] wrote, because 'whoever is the most outraged wins.' " And the following quote seems to summarize the essence of what makes cyberbullying such a serious problem:

> "It goes on and on," Kain said. "People are accused publicly, called out on social media. Pictures are posted. Rumors are circulated. Jobs are lost and reputations damaged. Sometimes the people being shamed are bad people. But always the shaming circumvents due process, precedes true justice, and serves mainly to inflate the sense of self-importance and egos of its progenitors." (Blake, 2019)

The incident also gives us hope that one person, standing up, can make a difference. He took the trouble to dig more deeply into the incident, determined that the young woman who was targeted had been falsely accused of racism, and began tweeting his support for her. He said, "The internet mob is so powerful. . . . For as much good as it can do—in the sense of fundraising and getting the word out—it can destroy, it can manipulate. It can literally ruin people's lives in a matter of seconds" (Blake, 2019). The efforts of this defender, Andrew Hallwarth, made an enormous difference, and it is my hope that we would all—including our politicians— follow his example.

Cam Juárez's Story

Cam Juárez is an outspoken and passionate activist for a variety of political causes, fighting for the rights of underrepresented minorities. He currently works for the National Park Service as a community engagement and outreach coordinator for Saguaro National Park, where his role includes increasing visitation rates for Latinos and other marginalized groups. He previously worked for several community development organizations and served a term on the school board for the city in which he

lives. His career has been devoted to increasing opportunities for under-
served populations.

Cam knows a lot about bullying. He describes himself as a survivor
(versus victim) of bullying that began at a very early age. He was born with
a heart defect and a visible physical deformity due to his exposure in utero
to pesticides sprayed on crops (and farmworkers) when his mother was
pregnant with him. When Cam started kindergarten in California with
his younger sister (Cam's enrollment in kindergarten was delayed a year so
the two could attend together), they were culturally Mexican in their language (Spanish only), poverty, customs, and experiences. For example,
they didn't know about the American practice of dressing in costumes on
Halloween and came to school that day dressed in regular clothes, a difference other children and adults noticed. His cultural differences plus his
visible disability made Cam a likely target for bullies, and as a child, he
was subjected to ongoing bullying by other children. Rather than succumb
and be a victim, Cam had been able to move beyond those experiences by
taking control of his own reactions. Perhaps his youthful experiences contributed to his dedication to efforts to improve opportunities and well-
being of traditionally underrepresented groups, donating time to many
initiatives and events, especially for youth. Of course, such personal convictions become political when voiced, and digital aggression thrives on
political division.

When he was college student, Cam met Raul Grijalva, who was then a
county supervisor running for reelection. At that time, the state legislature
was introducing a bill against bilingual education, and Cam attended a
panel on the topic that included Grijalva. After the presentation, a friend of
Cam's introduced him to Grijalva, telling him that Cam was a "student
activist." Grijalva must have been impressed, since he recruited Cam for a
position in the county's youth development services. He encouraged Cam
throughout his education, and Cam volunteered regularly in his campaign.
He has continued to be a supporter now that Grijalva is a U.S. Congressman from Arizona. When Cam originally met this politician over 20 years
ago, there was another group within the same political party from the same
community as Grijalva that had opposing agendas and viewpoints. These
two groups have been at odds over the years, and resentments have festered
to this day; the two groups have supported opposing candidates and have
publicly disagreed on a number of local hotbed issues.

Cam's role with the park service is to engage, educate, and encourage
diverse visitors to visit the park. Despite the fact that the park is located in
an area with a large Latinx population, very few regularly visit or have
ever visited the park. In collaboration with other employees at the park,
Cam's initiatives have significantly improved visits by that demographic,
and he has also become a dedicated protector of the national environment.

In the park where Cam works (and elsewhere in the region), there is a non-native grass species that is invasive and difficult to eradicate. The grass crowds out native plants, using precious water that those plants need to survive and increases fire danger in the park. As a result, the park service has worked to remove the buffalo grass in the region, with some success thanks to the assistance of volunteers. However, the size of the parks, and the remoteness and difficult terrain in some areas where the grass flourishes, makes it too dangerous for volunteers (and workers) to pull the grass by hand. As a result, the Park Service regional administration decided to use aerially distributed herbicides to eradicate the dangerous invasive species.

There is a local blogger (and social media user) aligned with the opposing political camp, and who apparently harbors animosity toward Cam dating back many years, who seized upon the practice mandated by senior regional park service officials to launch an assault on Cam. The blogger takes every opportunity to call out perceived wrongs enacted by Cam and has taken to ad hominem attacks that are particularly offensive. The blogger (threesonorans.org) attacked Cam for not publicly opposing the National Park Service—mandated directive to use herbicides, calling attention to his birth defects and mentioning Cam's eight-year- old son (who also has a genetic heart condition). The blogger called Cam a hypocrite for working for an agency that uses herbicides despite the serious consequences Cam had experienced due to their use. Cam believes mentioning his son's condition was the digital equivalent of a below-the-belt punch that demonstrates that the vitriol is about more than political differences.

Although the Three Sonorans blogger is a persistent digital aggressor toward Cam, he is not the only one. A local educational issue that has generated heated disagreements in the community is that of a Mexican American Studies curriculum that was implemented in high schools in the school district years ago. Conservatives adamantly opposed this program, and worked to have it banned. (It has now been approved for reinstatement after judicial decision dismissing the ban). Cam was a strong supporter of that program, and as such was attacked by conservative groups that resorted to such tactics as Photoshopping images to present Cam in a negative light. Cam is clear that the aggressors are a small but very vocal group who not only come from an opposing political view but appear to be anti-Mexican American in their posts.

Whether the cyberbully in chief's behavior has directly influenced Cam's detractors is impossible to determine. However, there was one incident that suggests that Trump's modeling has had an effect that occurred very shortly after Trump mimicked a disabled reporter's gestures. At a live radio talk show, observers contacted Cam afterward to report that during the interview, Cam's opponents on the school board were imitating his physical gestures, clearly mocking his disability. While not visible to listeners, or posted online, this illustrates the severity of the behaviors directly against Cam.

Just as he survived childhood bullying, Cam has not allowed the digital aggression to defeat him or to dampen his enthusiasm for important causes, especially those that involve the Latinx population. He carefully considers any online posts so that he models how to engage in a more civil discourse about political and other topics. He has a career and family to protect, and is judicious about what he shares in public spaces. He does not respond to character attacks.

What Cam's story highlights is how political issues readily become personal. It seems that when political disagreements occur, they easily devolve into personal antagonisms. Once that occurs, the use of irrelevant personal characteristics as targets of the hostility seems to follow. People who are public figures (as is Cam) become focal points for the expression of anger and bitterness whose origin may be only tangentially related to the current tension. The easy access to online platforms allows such anger to be transmitted and disseminated, often encouraging others to join the bandwagon of abuse.

John Doe's Story

Several concerns about mental illness have become political hot-button issues. Should it be covered by medical insurance? How should treatment facilities be funded? Should mentally ill persons in the prison system be released to more appropriate setting?

A bit of history might be helpful here. In the 1970s, there was a movement to de-institutionalize the mentally ill who were often warehoused in institutions (sometimes for life) with little or no attempts at treatment. Once that goal of de-institutionalization was realized, the expectation was that persons with mental illness would receive treatment in the community from community agencies, and live in group homes or other community settings. Unfortunately, the community agencies have not been able to accommodate the numbers requiring services nor has an equitable system for financing these services been devised. Thus, funding for mental health services, expansion of existing services, and insurance plans that consider mental illness to be on a par with physical illness in terms of coverage have all been debated at state and national levels.

The details in the following story are disguised in order to protect the privacy of the individual. The information was provided by the person's parent. As a young child, John Doe appeared to be like other children, was gregarious, and had friends. In retrospect, the parent noted that John never engaged in creative play on his own. His parents divorced when he was 10, which was quite traumatic for John. The divorce resulted in relocating to a new, larger city, with concomitant adjustment challenges, and soon John began experimenting with marijuana.

John Doe was diagnosed with schizoaffective disorder when he was in his early 20s and a college student. He had displayed early symptoms when he was younger, but they increased and drew the attention of students and others on campus. At the time he was attending university, he himself did not acknowledge that he had a mental illness. A concerned professor, however, was the one who first recognized that John's behavior was likely associated with mental illness, and referred him to the university's counseling center, where the diagnosis was made and treatment began. The dean of students worked closely with John to assist him in completing his degree.

John was eventually prescribed a variety of psychotropic medications to control his symptoms, and was seen for counseling at a community mental health agency. The medications prescribed need to be taken as scheduled and closely monitored; missing doses could result in symptom elevation. That happened on a number of occasions in John's life.

During college and afterward, John adopted the persona of a businessman, dressing in suit and tie and carrying a briefcase. John's communication was disorganized and tangential, and sometimes involved his delusions (e.g., he commanded a fleet of nuclear submarines). He patronized local cafes and coffee shops, where he might mutter to himself while waiting in line, and when it was his turn to order, turn away and leave without purchasing anything. His movements were very stylized and rigid, he speed-walked at times, and these behaviors attracted attention from students.

Doe Sr. learned from a colleague that a Facebook group called the Documentary of a Fake Business Man (FBM) had been created; at one point there were 947 members. Members would post sightings—time, location, attire, and so on. It appears it was a bit of a "Where's Waldo?" activity, but numerous photos and some video were included. One ongoing point of fascination was the contents of this briefcase, with various posters speculating about possible items. The posts uniformly pointed out the oddities in John's presentation or behavior, and included absurdities such as "he was heading east (where Pakistan is located) a few Sunday nights ago and the next day bin laden is dead." A Tumblr post also chronicled FBM's location and described the writer's "adventure" following him around and taking photos. A focus on many posts was whether or not he was seen carrying his briefcase. Buried on the site are two important posts: The creator of the group identified himself and said his purpose was not to make fun of John but "to learn about him and document his interactions around campus." This was a reply to a poster who was close to John during middle and high school, and was disturbed by the chronicle of John's "descent into madness." Those concerns were apparently disregarded by the rest of the group, as subsequent posts continued to report sightings and comment on his unusual behaviors. Another member of the group came to John's defense, suggesting that members of the group should leave John alone. His rationale was that potential employers could discover that members of the group were intolerant of people with "special needs." The few other posts suggesting that perhaps the existence of the group and its goal are inappropriate tended to be ignored or dismissed. An illustrative comment: "hahaha I just wasted my life making fun of someone I don't even know but for some reason it makes me feel good to rip on him for being such a weirdo." She concludes the post with "so I say plz let him be."

John's parent contacted the administrator of the Facebook page, who used his real name, and found him to be quite contrite. Doe Sr. made several attempts to get the group removed from Facebook, but since it was not his site, nor was he the one being mistreated, he had no authority. Over time it was taken down, and Doe wonders if the page administrator himself reconsidered and took it down.

Doe does not know if John ever saw the FB group or read the posts, or how he might respond if he had. Given his mental illness, which includes paranoia, Doe did not alert John nor did he ask him about it, fearing that it would cause more distress. It is also true that John's illness and its manifestations resulted in interactions with police and he was banned from certain locations in his community due to his disruptive behavior. Does this entitle others to make sport of documenting sightings, taking photos, posting those, and encouraging commentary? At the least, this suggests a lack of understanding of mental illness, and a callousness that is all too prevalent in today's society. It also shows that the hurt extends beyond the target—in this case, John's parent, and indirectly harms all persons with mental illness, making of their condition a joking matter.

References

Aced-Toledano, C. (2013, July 3). *Web 2.0: The origin of the word that has changed the way we understand public relations.* Presentation at the PR2013 Conference, Barcelona, Spain. Retrieved from https://www.researchgate.net/publication/266672416_Web_20_the_origin_of_the_word_that_has_changed_the_way_we_understand_public_relations

Akers, R. L. (2011). *Social learning and social structure: A general theory of crime and deviance.* New Brunswick, NJ: Transaction Publishers.

Anderson, M., Perrin, A., & Jiang, J. (2018, March 5). *11% of Americans don't use the internet. Who are they?* Washington, DC: Pew Research Center. Retrieved from http://www.pewresearch.org/fact-tank/2018/03/05/some-americans-dont-use-the-internet-who-are-they/

Anderson, M., & Toor, S. (2018, October 11). How social media users have discussed sexual harassment since #MeToo went viral. *FactTank.* Retrieved from https://www.pewresearch.org/fact-tank/2018/10/11/how-social-media-users-have-discussed-sexual-harassment-since-metoo-went-viral/

Avitabile, R. (2019, March 26). Embattled El Cajon City Councilman Ben Kalasho resigns. *NBC News San Diego.* Retrieved from https://www.nbcsandiego.com/news/local/Embattled-El-Cajon-City-Councilman-Ben-Kalasho-Announces-Resignation-507711351.html

Baker, K. J. M. (2016). Here's the powerful letter the Stanford victim read to her attacker. *BuzzFeed News.* Retrieved from https://www.buzzfeednews.com/article/katiejmbaker/heres-the-powerful-letter-the-stanford-victim-read-to-her-ra

Bandura, A. (1973). *Aggression: A social learning analysis.* New York, NY: Prentice-Hall.

Bandura, A. (1976). *Social learning theory.* New York, NY: Prentice-Hall.

Bandura, A. (1999). Moral disengagement in the perpetration of inhuman-ities. *Personality and Social Psychology Review, 3*(3), 193–209.

Bandura, A. (2002). Selective moral disengagement in the exercise of moral agency. *Journal of Moral Education, 31*(2), 101–119.

Bandura, A. (Ed.). (2017). *Psychological modeling: Conflicting theories.* New York, NY: Routledge.

Bandura, A., Barbaranelli, C., Caprara, G. V., & Pastorelli, C. (1996). Mech-anisms of moral disengagement in the exercise of moral agency. *Journal of Personality and Social Psychology, 71*(2), 364.

Baron, R. A., & Richardson, D. R. (1994). *Human aggression* (2nd ed.). New York, NY: Plenum Press.

Barron, B. (2019). 25 stunning WordPress facts you need to know today. *Who Is Hosting This?* Retrieved from https://www.whoishostingthis .com/compare/wordpress/stats/

Barron, J., & Hoban, P. (1998, January 28). Public lives, dueling soaps. *The New York Times.* Retrieved from https://www.nytimes.com/1998/ 01/28/nyregion/public-lives-dueling-soaps.html?sec=&spon

Bates, S. (2017). Revenge porn and mental health: A qualitative analysis of the mental health effects of revenge porn on female survivors. *Fem-inist Criminology, 12*(1), 22–42.

Bauman, S. A. (2010). Cyberbullying in a rural intermediate school: An exploratory study. *Journal of Early Adolescence, 30*(6), 803–833.

Bauman, S. A., Underwood, M.K., & Card, N. (2013). Definitions: Another perspective and a proposal for beginning with cyberaggression. In S. Bauman, J., Walker, & D. Cross (Eds.), *Principles of Cyberbullying Research: Definition, Methods, and Measures* (pp. 87–93). New York, NY: Routledge.

Begley, P. (2017, October 9). Alt-right speaker Milo Yiannopoulos seeks to "reveal hypocrisy through ridicule." *Sydney Morning Herald.* Retrieved from https://www.smh.com.au/business/companies/altright-speaker-milo-yiannopoulos-seeks-to-reveal-hypocrisy-through-ridicule-2017 1009-gywu1r.html

Benko, R. (2017, June 30). Trigger warning, how the trolls occupied politics and what to do about it. *Forbes.* Retrieved from https://www.forbes .com/sites/ralphbenko/2017/06/30/trigger-warning-how-the-trolls-occupied-politics-and-what-to-do-about-it/#3a7b93c6bdfa

Berkowitz, L. (1993). *Aggression: Its causes, consequences, and control.* McGraw-Hill series in social psychology. New York, NY: McGraw-Hill.

Bethel School District #43 v. Fraser, 478 U.S. 675 (1986).

Bishop, J. (2014). Digital teens and the "antisocial network": Prevalence of troublesome online youth groups and internet trolling in

Great Britain. *International Journal of E-Politics (IJEP)*, *5*(3), 1–15.

Blake, J. (2019, May 25). How an internet mob falsely painted a Chipotle employee as racist. *CNN*. Retrieved from https://www.cnn.com/2019/05/25/us/false-racism-internet-mob-chipotle-video/index.html

Bronfenbrenner, U. (1979). *The ecology of human development*. Cambridge, MA: Harvard University Press.

Bronfenbrenner, U. (1995). Developmental ecology through space and time: A future perspective. In P. Moen, G. H. Elder, Jr., & K. Lüscher (Eds.), *Examining lives in context: Perspectives on the ecology of human development* (pp. 619–647). Washington, DC: American Psychological Association.

Bronfenbrenner, U. (2005). *Making human beings human: Bioecological perspectives on human development*. Thousand Oaks, CA: Sage.

Brown, A. (2018, July 26). Most Americans say higher ed is heading in wrong direction, but partisans disagree on why. *Pew Research Center*. Retrieved from https://www.pewresearch.org/fact-tank/2018/07/26/most-americans-say-higher-ed-is-heading-in-wrong-direction-but-partisans-disagree-on-why/

Brown, K. V. (2017, July 24). From LOL to LULZ, the evolution of the internet troll over 24 years. *Splinter*. Retrieved from https://splinternews.com/from-lol-to-lulz-the-evolution-of-the-internet-troll-o-1793855652

Buckels, E. E., Trapnell, P. D., & Paulhus, D. L. (2014). Trolls just want to have fun. *Personality and Individual Differences*, *67*, 97–102.

Bullingham, L., & Vasconcelos, A. C. (2013). "The presentation of self in the online world": Goffman and the study of online identities. *Journal of Information Science*, *39*(1), 101–112.

Bump, P. (2016, August 19). For which of these two dozen things is Donald Trump finally expressing regret? *Washington Post*. Retrieved from https://www.washingtonpost.com/news/the-fix/wp/2016/08/19/for-which-of-these-two-dozen-things-is-donald-trump-finally-expressing-regret/?utm_term=.95bb439a9cf1

Buncombe, A. (2018, January 18). How Donald Trump's use of Twitter has changed the US presidency. *Independent*. Retrieved from https://www.independent.co.uk/news/world/americas/us-politics/the-twitter-president-how-potus-changed-social-media-and-the-presidency-a8164161.html

Burroughs, B. (2013). FCJ-165 Obama trolling: Memes, salutes and an agonistic politics in the 2012 presidential election. *Fibreculture Journal*, *22*, 257–276.

Burt, A., & Alhabash, S. (2017). Illuminating the nomological network of digital aggression: Results from two studies. *Aggressive Behavior, 44,* 125–135.

Carson, D. (2016, August 18). Vermont legislators react strongly to "racist" tweet at Bennington's Rep. Kiah Morris. *The Berkshire Eagle.* Retrieved from https://www.berkshireeagle.com/stories/vermont-legislators-react-strongly-to-racist-tweet-at-benningtons-rep-kiah-morris, 180588

Chaplinsky v. New Hampshire. (n.d.). *Oyez.* Retrieved from https://www.oyez.org/cases/1940-1955/315us568

Chatzakou, D., Kourtellis, N., Blackburn, J., De Cristofaro, E., Stringhini, G., & Vakali, A. (2017, June). Mean birds: Detecting aggression and bullying on twitter. In *Proceedings of the 2017 ACM on Web Science Conference* (pp. 13–22).

Cheung, C. M., Wong, R. Y. M., & Chan, T. K. (2016). Online disinhibition: Conceptualization, measurement, and relation to aggressive behaviors. *Proceedings of the International Conference on Information Systems.*

Cialdini, R. B. (2007). Descriptive social norms as underappreciated sources of social control. *Psychometrika, 72*(2), 263.

Cillizza, C. (2018, November 29). Donald Trump, Internet troll. *CNN.* Retrieved from https://www.cnn.com/2018/11/28/politics/donald-trump-internet-troll/index.html

Cohen v. California, 403 U.S. 15 (1971).

Cohen v. California. (n.d.). *Oyez.* Retrieved from https://www.oyez.org/cases/1970/299

Comello, M. L. G. (2009). William James on "possible selves": Implications for studying identity in communication contexts. *Communication Theory, 19*(3), 337–350.

Courtney. (n.d.). 28-year-old congressional candidate won't let slut-shaming make her quit. *Feministing.* Retrieved from http://feministing.com/2010/10/12/28-year-old-congressional-candidate-wont-let-slut-shaming-make-her-quit/

Coyne, I., Farley, S., Axtell, C., Sprigg, C., Best, L., & Kwok, O. (2017). Understanding the relationship between experiencing workplace cyberbullying, employee mental strain and job satisfaction: A dysempowerment approach. *The International Journal of Human Resource Management, 28*(7), 945–972.

Craker, N., & March, E. (2016). The dark side of Facebook®: The Dark Tetrad, negative social potency, and trolling behaviours. *Personality and Individual Differences, 102,* 79–84.

Cranley, E. (2018, May 3). 9 members of Congress who were forced out of office by sexual misconduct scandals. *Business Insider.* Retrieved from https://www.businessinsider.com/congress-sex-scandals-forced-out-of-office-2018-5#rep-joe-barton-of-texas-republican-6

Crick, N. R. (1996). The role of overt aggression, relational aggression, and prosocial behavior in the prediction of children's future social adjustment. *Child Development, 67*(5), 2317–2327.

Crick, N. R., & Dodge, K. A. (1994). A review and reformulation of social information-processing mechanisms in children's social adjustment. *Psychological Bulletin, 115*(1), 74–101.

Crowe, M. (2016, August 5). "Revenge porn" can devastate victims—And their employers. *Puget Sound Business Journal.* Retrieved from https://www.bizjournals.com/seattle/blog/techflash/2016/08/revenge-porn-can-devastate-victims-and-their.html

Cuevas, J. A. (2018). A new reality? The far right's use of cyberharassment against academics. *Academe, 104*(1). Retrieved from https://www.aaup.org/article/new-reality-far-rights-use-cyberharassment-against-academics#.XOc5MS_Mw_V

Daum, M. (2013, March 7). Online's "nasty effect." *Los Angeles Times.* Retrieved from http://articles.latimes.com/2013/mar/07/opinion/la-oe-daum-comments-nasty-effect-20130307

David, L. (2018, November 19). Just want to point out all the kids in school with the last name #Schiff getting bullied and name called #Schitt today because of the president of the US. I know because my neices are Schiffs. #BeBest. [Tweet]. Retrieved from https://twitter.com/Laurie_David/status/1064489326413840384

Davison, C. B., & Stein, C. H. (2014). The dangers of cyberbullying. *North American Journal of Psychology, 16*(3). Retrieved from https://link-gale-com.ezproxy3.library.arizona.edu/apps/doc/A392177618/AONE?u=uarizona_main&sid=AONE&xid=472a8968

DeNardis, L., & Hackl, A. M. (2015). Internet governance by social media. *Telecommunications Policy, 39*(9), 761–770.

Dennen, J.M.G. van der. (2005). Theories of aggression: Frustration-aggression (F-A) theory. *Default Journal Holland.* Retrieved from https://www.rug.nl/research/portal/files/2908668/A-FAT.pdf

Dockray, H. (2018, October 23). Politicians are trolling to win the midterms. Some of it is actually good. *Mashable.* Retrieved from https://mashable.com/article/candidates-troll-midterms/#k3H4YCLkeaqq

Dodge, K. A. (1986). A social information processing model of social competence in children. In M. Perlmutter (Ed.), *Minnesota symposium on child psychology* (Vol. 18, pp. 77–125). Hillsdale, NJ: Erlbaum.

Dollard, J., Miller, N. E., Doob, L. W., Mowrer, O. H., & Sears, R. R. (1939). *Frustration and aggression.* New Haven, CT: Yale University Press.

Dow, B. J. (2017). Taking Trump seriously: Persona and presidential politics in 2016. *Women's Studies in Communication, 40*(2), 136–139.

Duggan, M. (2017, July). *Online harassment 2017.* Retrieved from https://www.pewinternet.org/2017/07/11/online-harassment-2017/

Durkin, E. (2018, September 19). Christine Blasey Ford's life "turned upside down" after accusing Kavanaugh. *The Guardian.* Retrieved from https://www.theguardian.com/us-news/2018/sep/19/christine-blasey-ford-brett-kavanaugh-sexual-assault-accuser-threats

Earle, S. (2017, October 14). How social media is being used by governments to settle scores and silence critics. *Newsweek.* Retrieved from https://www.newsweek.com/trolls-bots-and-fake-news-dark-and-mysterious-world-social-media-manipulation-682155

Eckstrand, N. (2018). The ugliness of trolls: Comparing the methodologies of the alt-right and the Ku Klux Klan. *Cosmopolitan Civil Societies: An Interdisciplinary Journal, 10*(3), 41–62.

Editorial Board. (2018, August 2). If not for the outspoken women . . . *Chicago Tribune.* Retrieved from https://www.chicagotribune.com/news/opinion/editorials/ct-edit-sauer-sex-harassment-springfield-20180801-story.html

Elliott, J. K. (2019, March 19). No one reported New Zealand shooting video while it was live, Facebook says. *Global News.* Retrieved from https://globalnews.ca/news/5071050/new-zealand-mosque-shooting-video-facebook-live/

Ellison, N. B., Hancock, J. T., & Toma, C. L. (2012). Profile as promise: A framework for conceptualizing veracity in online dating self-presentations. *New Media & Society, 14*(1), 45–62.

Fisher, M. (2012, August 22). After the scandal: Krystal Ball's transparent life. *The Cut.* Retrieved from https://www.thecut.com/2012/08/krystal-balls-transparent-life.html

Flynn, M. (2018, June 6). Brock Turner: Judge who gave lenient sentence to Stanford student who sexually assaulted unconscious woman removed by voters in recall election. *Independent.* Retrieved from https://www.independent.co.uk/news/world/americas/brock-turner-judge-aaron-persky-removed-recall-election-stanford-rape-sentence-a8385681.html

Gajanan, M. (2018, March 21). Melania Trump is "well-aware of the criticism over her anti-cyberbullying campaign." *TIME.* Retrieved from http://time.com/5208298/melania-trump-anti-cyberbullying-campaign/

García-Rapp, F., & Roca-Cuberes, C. (2017). Being an online celebrity: Norms and expectations of YouTube's beauty community. *First Monday, 22*(7). Retrieved from https://firstmonday.org/ojs/index.php/fm/article/view/7788/6331

Gardner, A. (2018, October 8). Christine Blasey Ford is still receiving death threats after Kavanaugh confirmation. *Glamour.* Retrieved from https://www.glamour.com/story/christine-blasey-ford-receiving-death-threats-unable-return-home-kavanaugh-confirmation

Gardner, D., O'Driscoll, M., Cooper-Thomas, H. D., Roche, M., Bentley, T., Catley, B., . . . & Trenberth, L. (2016). Predictors of workplace bullying and cyber-bullying in New Zealand. *International Journal of Environmental Research and Public Health, 13*(5), 448.

Goffman, E. (1959). *The presentation of self in everyday life.* New York, NY: Doubleday.

Gottfried, J., & Shearer, E. (2017, September 7). *Americans' online news use is closing in on TV news use.* Washington, DC: Pew Research Center. Retrieved from http://www.pewresearch.org/fact-tank/2017/09/07/americans-online-news-use-vs-tv-news-use/

Green, M. (2018, January 24). No comment! Why more news sites are dumping their comment sections. *KQED News.* Retrieved from https://www.kqed.org/lowdown/29720/no-comment-why-a-growing-number-of-news-sites-are-dumping-their-comment-sections

Grygiel, J., & Brown, N. (2019). Are social media companies motivated to be good corporate citizens? Examination of the connection between corporate social responsibility and social media safety? *Telecommunications Policy, 43*, 445–460.

Gunia, A. (2019, May 14). Facebook tightens live-stream rules in response to the Christchurch massacre. *TIME.* Retrieved from http://time.com/5589478/facebook-tightens-live-stream-rules-in-response-to-the-christchurch-massacre/

Gurr, T. R. (1970). *Why men rebel.* Princeton, NJ: Princeton University Press.

Gurr, T. R. (2011). *Why men rebel: 40th anniversary edition.* Oxford, UK: Routledge.

Haldevang, M. D. (2018, October 3). Russian trolls and bots are flooding Twitter with Ford-Kavanaugh disinformation. *Quartz.* Retrieved from https://qz.com/1409102/russian-trolls-and-bots-are-flooding-twitter-with-ford-kavanaugh-disinformation/

Hardaker, C. (2010). Trolling in asynchronous computer-mediated communication: From user discussions to academic definitions. *Journal of Politeness Research. Language, Behaviour, Culture, 6*(2), 215–242.

Hayes, C., & Bacon, J. (2018, June 6). Judge Aaron Persky, who gave Brock Turner lenient sentence in rape case, recalled from office. *USA Today.* Retrieved from https://www.usatoday.com/story/news/2018/06/06/judge-aaron-persky-who-gave-brock-turners-lenient-sentence-sanford-rape-case-recalled/674551002/

Hazelwood School District v. Kuhlmeier, 484 U.S. 260 (1988).

Holfeld, B., & Grabe, M. (2012). Middle school students' perceptions of and responses to cyber bullying. *Journal of Educational Computing Research, 46*(4), 395–413.

Hong, S., & Nadler, D. (2011, June). Does the early bird move the polls?: The use of the social media tool "Twitter" by US politicians and its impact on public opinion. In *Proceedings of the 12th Annual International Digital Government Research Conference: Digital Government Innovation in Challenging Times* (pp. 182–186). ACM.

Huang, F. L., & Cornell, D. G. (2019). School teasing and bullying after the presidential election. *Educational Researcher, 48*(2), 69–83. https://doi.org/10.3102/0013189X18820291

Hughes, A., & Lam, O. (2017, August 21). *Highly ideological members of Congress have more Facebook followers that moderates do.* Washington, DC: *Pew Research Center.* Retrieved from https://www.pewresearch.org/fact-tank/2017/08/21/highly-ideological-members-of-congress-have-more-facebook-followers-than-moderates-do/

Hughes, A., & Van Kessel, P. (2018, July 18). *"Anger" topped "love" when Facebook users reacted to lawmakers' posts after 2016 election.* Washington, DC: Pew Research Center. Retrieved from https://www.pewresearch.org/fact-tank/2018/07/18/anger-topped-love-facebook-after-2016-election/

Jenkins, H. (2008, September 10). Photoshop for democracy revisited: The Sarah Palin file, confessions of an ACA-Fan [Blog post]. Retrieved from http://henryjenkins.org/blog/2008/09/photoshop_for_democracy_revisi.html

Johnson, G. M., & Puplampu, K. P. (2008). Internet use during childhood and the ecological techno-subsystem. *Canadian Journal of Learning and Technology/La revue canadienne de l'apprentissage et de la technologie, 34*(1), 19–28.

Joinson, A. (1998). Causes and implications of disinhibited behavior on the Internet. In J. Gackenbach (Ed.), *Psychology and the internet: Intrapersonal, interpersonal, and transpersonal implications* (pp. 43–60). San Diego, CA, US: Academic Press.

Joinson, A. N. (2007). Disinhibition and the internet. In J. Gackenbach (Ed.), *Psychology and the internet: Intrapersonal, interpersonal, and transpersonal implications* (pp. 75–92). San Diego, CA: Academic Press.

Jordan, M. A. (2014, February 4). What's in a meme? *Richard Dawkins Foundation for Reason & Science.* Retrieved from https://www.richarddawkins.net/2014/02/whats-in-a-meme/

Jung, C. G., McGuire, W. Read, H., Fordham, M., & Adler, G. (1969). *The collected works of C.G. Jung, vol. 9, part 1: Archetypes and the collective unconscious.* London, UK: Routledge.

Jussinoja, T. (2018). Life-cycle of internet trolls (Master's thesis, University of Jyväskylä). Retrieved from https://jyx.jyu.fi/handle/123456789/57411

Karrpi, T. (2013). FCJ-166 "Change name to no one. Like people's status" Facebook trolling and managing online personas. *Fibreculture Journal, 22.* Retrieved from http://twentytwo.fibreculturejournal.org/fcj-166-change-name-to-no-one-like-peoples-status-facebook-trolling-and-managing-online-personas/

Kavakci, E., & Kraeplin, C. R. (2017). Religious beings in fashionable bodies: The online identity construction of hijabi social media personalities. *Media, Culture & Society, 39*(6), 850–868.

Keays, A. (2019, January 4). Morris "victim of racial harassment," but AG not filing criminal charges. *VTDigger. Retrieved from* https://vtdig ger.org/2019/01/14/donovan-says-no-evidence-prosecutions-kiah-morris-case/

Kelly, E. (2018, March 27). Monica Lewinsky decries the growing culture of public shaming. *USA Today.* Retrieved from https://www.usato day.com/story/news/politics/2018/03/27/monica-lewinsky-decries-growing-culture-public-shaming/461738002/

Kim, J., & Lee, J. E. R. (2011). The Facebook paths to happiness: Effects of the number of Facebook friends and self-presentation on subjective well-being. *CyberPsychology, Behavior, and Social Networking, 14*(6), 359–364.

Kopecký, K. (2016). Misuse of web cameras to manipulate children within the so-called webcam trolling. *Telematics and Informatics, 33*(1), 1–7.

Kowalski, R. M., Giumetti, G. W., Schroeder, A. N., & Reese, H. (2012). Cyberbullying among college students: Evidence from multiple domains of college life. In C. Wankel & L. Wankel (Eds.), *Misbehavior online in higher education* (pp. 293–321). Bingley, UK: Emerald.

Krieg, G. (2018, October 16). Who's Trump attacking on Twitter? *CNN.* Retrieved from https://www.cnn.com/2018/08/18/politics/who-trump-attacks-insults-on-twitter/index.html

Langlois, G., & Slane, A. (2017). Economies of reputation: The case of revenge porn. *Communication and Critical/Cultural Studies, 14*(2), 120–138.

Lapidot-Lefler, N., & Barak, A. (2012). Effects of anonymity, invisibility, and lack of eye-contact on toxic online disinhibition. *Computers in Human Behavior, 28*(2), 434–443.

Lawson, C. E. (2018). *Platform feminism: Celebrity culture and activism in the digital age* (Doctoral dissertation, University of Michigan). Retrieved from ProQuest Dissertations & Theses Global. (2166297121).

Lewinsky, M. (2018, February 25). Monica Lewinsky: Emerging from the "house of the Gaslight" in the age of #MeToo. *Vanity Fair.* Retrieved from https://www.vanityfair.com/news/2018/02/monica-lewinsky-in-the-age-of-metoo

Lewis, P. (2018, December 18). Vermont's only black woman lawmaker pulls out of race in wake of online threats. *Huffington Post*. Retrieved from https://www.huffingtonpost.com/entry/vermonts-only-black-woman-lawmaker-pulls-out-of-race-in-wake-of-online-threats_us_5b848992e4b0162f471bb0ee

Li, Q. (2007). New bottle but old wine: A research of cyberbullying in schools. *Computers in Human Behavior, 23*(4), 1777–1791.

Lin, H., & Wang, H. (2014). Avatar creation in virtual worlds: Behaviors and motivations. *Computers in Human Behavior, 34*, 213–218.

Lorenz, K. (1966). *On aggression.* New York, NY: Harcourt, Brace & World.

Lorenz, T. (2019, March 15). The shooter's manifesto was designed to troll. *The Atlantic.* Retrieved from https://www.theatlantic.com/technology/archive/2019/03/the-shooters-manifesto-was-designed-to-troll/585058/

Lowry, P. B., Zhang, J., Wang, C., & Siponen, M. (2016). Why do adults engage in cyberbullying on social media? An integration of online disinhibition and deindividuation effects with the social structure and social learning model. *Information Systems Research, 27*(4), 962–986.

MacKinnon, C. A. (2019, March 24). Where #MeToo came from, and where it's going. *The Atlantic.* Retrieved from https://www.theatlantic.com/ideas/archive/2019/03/catharine-mackinnon-what-metoo-has-changed/585313/

Maheshwari, S., & Herrman, J. (2018, August 13). This company keeps lies about Sandy Hook on the web. *The New York Times.* Retrieved from https://www.nytimes.com/2018/08/13/business/media/sandy-hook-conspiracies-leonard-pozner.html

Marantz, A. (2016, October 24). Trolls for Trump. *The New Yorker.* Retrieved from https://www.newyorker.com/magazine/2016/10/31/trolls-for-trump

Marantz, A. (2017, August 17). Is Trump trolling the White House press corps? *The New Yorker.* Retrieved from https://www.newyorker.com/magazine/2017/03/20/is-trump-trolling-the-white-house-press-corps?reload=true

Marantz, A. (2018, August 13). Trolls for Trump. *The New Yorker.* Retrieved from https://www.newyorker.com/magazine/2016/10/31/trolls-for-trump

March, E., Grieve, R., Marrington, J., & Jonason, P. K. (2017). Trolling on Tinder® (and other dating apps): Examining the role of the Dark Tetrad and impulsivity. *Personality and Individual Differences, 110*, 139–143.

Marshall, P. D. (2014). Persona studies: Mapping the proliferation of the public self. *Journalism, 15*(2), 153–170.

Marshall, P. D., & Henderson, N. (2016). Political persona 2016—An introduction. *Persona Studies, 2*(2), 1–18.

Marwick, A. E. (2013). *Status update: Celebrity, publicity, and branding in the social media age.* New Haven, CT: Yale University Press.

Marwick, A. E., & Boyd, D. (2011). To see and be seen: Celebrity practice on Twitter. *Convergence, 17*(2), 139–158.

Marwick, A. E., & Lewis, R. (2017, May 15). *Media manipulation and disinformation online.* New York, NY: Data & Society Research Institute.

Merrin, W. (2019). President troll: Trump, 4Chan and Memetic warfare. In C. Happer, A. Hoskins, & W. Merrin (Eds.), *Trump's media war* (pp. 201–226). Cham, Switzerland: Springer Nature Switzerland AG.

Meter, D. J., & Bauman, S. (2015). When sharing is a bad idea: The effects of online social network engagement and sharing passwords with friends on cyberbullying involvement. *Cyberpsychology, Behavior, and Social Networking, 18*(8), 437–442.

Meter, D. J., & Bauman, S. A. (2018). Moral disengagement about cyberbullying and parental monitoring: Effects on traditional bullying and victimization via cyberbullying involvement. *Journal of Early Adolescence, 38*(3), 303–326.

Metz, C., & Satariono, A. (2019, May 14). Facebook restricts live streaming after New Zealand shooting. *The New York Times.* Retrieved from https://www.nytimes.com/2019/05/14/technology/facebook-live-violent-content.html?action=click&module=Latest&pgtype=Homepage

Millay, K. (2017, June 4). We need fraternity men to do a lot more than "walk a mile in her shoes." *Everyday Feminism Magazine.* Retrieved from https://everydayfeminism.com/2017/06/fraternity-men-need-to-do-more/

Miller, H. (2018, November 28). Melania Trump on "Be Best" anti-cyberbullying campaign: Sometimes you have to fight back. *Huffington Post.* Retrieved from https://www.huffpost.com/entry/melania-trump-be-best-cyberbullying-fight-back_n_5bfecfabe4b0e254c926d229

Moore, C., Barbour, K., & Lee, K. (2017). Five dimensions of online persona. *Persona Studies, 3*(1), 1–11.

Morse v. Frederick, __ U.S. __ (2007). (g).

Müller, K., & Schwarz, C. (2018). Making America hate again? Twitter and hate crime under Trump. *SSRN Electronic Journal.* Retrieved from https://ssrn.com/abstract=3149103

Nelson, L. (2016. September 28). Why the Anti-Defamation League just put the Pepe the Frog meme on its hate symbols list. *Vox.* Retrieved from https://www.vox.com/2016/9/21/12893656/pepe-frog-donald-trump

Newport, F. (2018, May 16). Deconstructing Trump's use of Twitter. *Gallup.* Retrieved from https://news.gallup.com/poll/234509/deconstructing-trump-twitter.aspx

Nguyen, H. (2017). Americans think more should be done to combat cyberbullying. *YouGov.* Retrieved from https://today.yougov.com/topics/politics/articles-reports/2017/08/10/america-would-welcome-anti-cyberbullying-campaign-

Nickerson, R. S. (1998). Confirmation bias: A ubiquitous phenomenon in many guises. *Review of General Psychology, 2*(2), 175.

Osnos, E. (2016, June 19). The year of the political troll. *The New Yorker.* Retrieved from https://www.newyorker.com/news/daily-comment/the-year-of-the-political-troll

Perkins, H. W., Craig, D. W., & Perkins, J. M. (2011). Using social norms to reduce bullying: A research intervention among adolescents in five middle schools. *Group Processes & Intergroup Relations, 14*(5), 703–722.

Pew Research Center. (2018, February 5). *Demographics of mobile device ownership and adoption in the United States.* Washington, DC: Pew Research Center. Retrieved from http://www.pewinternet.org/fact-sheet/mobile/

Pfefferbaum, B., Newman, E., Nelson, S., Nitiéma, P., Pfefferbaum, R. L., & Rahman, R. (2014). Disaster media coverage and psychological outcomes: Descriptive findings in the extant research. *Current Psychiatry Reports, 16*(9), 1–7.

Phillips, W. (2011). LOLing at tragedy: Facebook trolls, memorial pages and resistance to grief online. *First Monday, 16*(12). Retrieved from https://uncommonculture.org/ojs/index.php/fm/article/view/3168/3115

Piotrowski, C. (2012). From workplace bullying to cyberbullying: The enigma of e-harassment in modern organizations. *Organization Development Journal, 30*(4), 44.

Poole, E. (2014). Hey girls, did you know? Slut-shaming on the internet needs to stop. *University of San Francisco Law Review, 48,* 221–262.

Pratt, G. (2018, September 8). Cruel online posts known as RIP trolling add to Tinley Park family's grief. *Chicago Tribune.* Retrieved from https://www.chicagotribune.com/suburbs/ct-xpm-2013-08-12-ct-met-rip-trolling-20130812-story.html

Privitera, C., & Campbell, M. A. (2009). Cyberbullying: The new face of workplace bullying? *CyberPsychology & Behavior, 12*(4), 395–400.

Protection for private blocking and screening of offensive material, 47 USC. § 230.

Quorum (2018) Report: Congress on social media. Preview of the 116th Congress Freshman Class Retrieved from https://readymag.com/u41777038/1235492/16/

Reicher, S. D., Spears, R., & Postmes, T. (1995). A social identity model of deindividuation phenomena. *European Review of Social Psychology, 6*(1), 161–198.

Riechers, A. (2012). My mourning junkie: Wailing at the Facebook wall. In *Workshop Memento Mori: Technology design for the end of life,* CHI 2012, Austin, May 2012. Retrieved from https://sites.google.com/site/chi2012eol/accepted-papers

Reinstein, M. (2019, January 16). I got death threats for writing a bad review of "Aquaman." *Huffington Post.* Retrieved from https://www.huffpost.com/entry/female-film-critic_n_5c3ce217e4b01c93e00c7fcf

Romm, T., & Harwell, D. (2019, May 15). White House declines to back Christchurch call to stamp out online extremism amid free speech concerns. *The Washington Post.* Retrieved from https://www.washingtonpost.com/technology/2019/05/15/white-house-will-not-signchristchurch-pact-stamp-out-online-extremism-amid-free-speech-concerns/?utm_term=.dcf7e63a7937&wpisrc=nl_most&wpmm=1

Roose, K. (2018, October 19). "Corrupt Chris" and "Two-faced Tammy": Candidates try their best Trump impressions. *The New York Times.* Retrieved from https://www.nytimes.com/2018/10/19/us/politics/corrupt-chris-and-two-faced-tammy-candidates-try-their-best-trump-impressions.html

Rosenberg, E. (2019, February 7). Trump's troop deployment strung "lethal" razor wire on the border. This city has had enough. *Washington Post.* Retrieved from https://www.washingtonpost.com/nation/2019/02/07/trumps-troop-deployment-strung-lethal-razor-wire-border-this-city-has-had-enough/?noredirect=on&utm_term=.931d0b55bd42

Roth v. United States, 354 U.S. 476 (1957).

Roy, J. (2016, October 11). How "Pepe the Frog" went from harmless to hate symbol. *Los Angeles Times.* Retrieved from https://www.latimes.com/politics/la-na-pol-pepe-the-frog-hate-symbol-20161011-snap-htmlstory.html

Rui, J., & Stefanone, M. A. (2013). Strategic self-presentation online: A cross-cultural study. *Computers in Human Behavior, 29*(1), 110–118.

Runions, K. C. (2013). Toward a conceptual model of motive and self-control in cyber-aggression: Rage, revenge, reward, and recreation. *Journal of Youth and Adolescence, 42*(5), 751–771.

Runions, K. C., Salmivalli, C., Shaw, T., Burns, S., & Cross, D. (2018). Beyond the reactive-proactive dichotomy: Rage, revenge, reward, and recreational aggression predict early high school bully and bully/victim status. *Aggressive Behavior, 44*(5), 501–511.

Samaha, A., Hayes, M., & Ansari, T. (2017, June 6). Kids are quoting Trump to bully their classmates and teachers don't know what to do about it. *BuzzFeedNews*. Retrieved from https://www.buzzfeednews.com/article/albertsamaha/kids-are-quoting-trump-to-bully-their-classmates

Sanfilippo, M. R., Fichman, P., & Yang, S. (2018). Multidimensionality of online trolling behaviors. *The Information Society, 34*(1), 27–39.

Sansone, R. A., & Sansone, L. A. (2015). Workplace bullying: A tale of adverse consequences. *Innovations in Clinical Neuroscience, 12*(1–2), 32.

Schenck v. United States. (n.d.). *Oyez*. Retrieved from https://www.oyez.org/cases/1900-1940/249us47

Schrecker, E. (2018). The AAUP in the age of Trump: When the rules have changed, how should the AAUP react? *Academe*. Retrieved from https://www.aaup.org/article/aaup-age-trump#.XOfH7C_Mw_U

Schultz, P. W., Nolan, J. M., Cialdini, R. B., Goldstein, N. J., & Griskevicius, V. (2007). The constructive, destructive, and reconstructive power of social norms. *Psychological Science, 18*(5), 429–434.

Seifullah, A. (2018, July 18). Revenge porn took my career. The law couldn't get it back. *Jezebel*. Retrieved from https://jezebel.com/revenge-porn-took-my-career-the-law-couldnt-get-it-bac-1827572768

Shane, S., & Blinder, A. (2019, January 7). Democrats faked online push to outlaw alcohol in Alabama race. *The New York Times*. Retrieved from https://www.nytimes.com/2019/01/07/us/politics/alabama-senate-facebook-roy-moore.html

Shapiro, B. (2010). *Brainwashed: How universities indoctrinate America's youth*. NY: HarperCollins.

Simon, M., & Sidner, S. (2019, May 15). A gunman slaughtered 11 Jewish worshippers. Then people hunted for hate online. *CNN*. Retrieved from https://www.cnn.com/2019/05/15/us/anti-semitic-searches-pittsburgh-poway-shootings-soh/index.html

Smith, D. (2014). Charlie is so "English"-like: Nationality and the branded celebrity person in the age of YouTube. *Celebrity Studies, 5*(3), 256–274.

Smith, J. (2017). The politician/celebrity and fan (girl) pleasure: The line between Queen Hillary and presidential candidate Clinton. *Persona Studies, 3*(2), 35–50.

Smith, S., & Watson, J. (2014). Virtually me: A toolbox about online self-presentation. *Identity Technologies: Constructing the Self Online*, 70–95.

Smyth, P. (2016, April 2). World view: Donald Trump uses social media to toxic effect. *Irish Times.* Retrieved from https://www.irishtimes .com/opinion/world-view-donald-trump-uses-social-media-to-toxic-effect-1.2595299

Soral, W., Bilewicz, M., & Winiewski, M. (2018). Exposure to hate speech increases prejudice through desensitization. *Aggressive Behavior, 44*(2), 136–146.

Spears, R. (2017). Social identity model of deindividuation effects. *The International Encyclopedia of Media Effects, vol. 9,* 1–9.

Statista.com. (2017, July). *Number of social media users worldwide 2010–2021.* Retrieved from https://www.statista.com/statistics/ 278414/number-of-worldwide-social-network-users/

Statista.com. (2019). Burson, Cohn & Wolfe; Twiplomacy. *Twitter accounts with the most followers worldwide as of April 2019 (in millions).* Retrieved from https://www.statista.com/statistics/273172/twitter-accounts-with-the-most-followers-worldwide/

Stewart, L. G., Arif, A., & Starbird, K. (2018, February). *Examining trolls and polarization with a retweet network.* Paper presented at MIS2: Misinformation and Misbehavior Mining on the Web, Del Rey, California. Retrieved from https://faculty.washington.edu/kstarbi/ examining-trolls-polarization.pdf

Stout. D. (2019). Social media statistics 2019: Top networks by the numbers. Retrieved from https://dustinstout.com/social-media-statistics/#google-plus-stats

Strangelove, M. (2010). *Watching YouTube: Extraordinary videos by ordinary people.* University of Toronto Press.

Suler, J. (2004). The online disinhibition effect. *Cyberpsychology & Behavior, 7*(3), 321–326.

Suler, J. (2005). The online disinhibition effect. *International Journal of Applied Psychoanalytic Studies, 2*(2), 184–188.

Suler, J. R. (2016). *Psychology of the digital age: Humans become electric.* Cambridge, UK: Cambridge University Press.

Sullivan, M. (2019, May 16). Trump won't stop coining nasty nicknames for his foes, but the media must stop amplifying them. *The Washington Post.* Retrieved from https://www.washingtonpost.com/life style/style/trump-wont-stop-coining-nasty-nicknames-for-his-foes—but-the-media-must-stop-amplifying-them/2019/05/15/ fa49cb52–7727–11e9-b3f5–5673edf2d127_story.html?utm_term= .1891c2e98214&wpisrc=nl_most&wpmm=1

Swearer, S. M., & Espelage, D. L. (2004). Introduction: A social-ecological framework of bullying among youth. In D. L. Espelage & S. M. Swearer (Eds.), *Bullying in American schools: A social-ecological perspective on prevention and intervention* (pp. 1–12). Mahwah, NJ: Lawrence Erlbaum Associates Publishers.

Swearer, S. M., & Espelage, D. L. (2011). Expanding the social-ecological framework of bullying among youth. In S. M. Swearer & D. L. Espelage (Eds.). *Bullying in North American Schools* (pp. 3–10). NY: Routledge.

Swisher, K. (2018, December 24). All text and no subtext: What will the historians of the future learn from the past week in Donald Trump's Twitter feed? *The New York Times.* Retrieved from https://www.nytimes.com/2018/12/24/opinion/trump-twitter-wall-shutdown.html

Telford, T. (2018, August 28). Someone posted photos of a young councilwoman in her underwear. She calls it "slut-shaming." *Chicago Tribune.* Retrieved from https://www.chicagotribune.com/opinion/commentary/ct-perspec-slut-shaming-women-political-candidates-0829-story.html

Terminiello v. Chicago, 337 US1, 1949. Retrieved from https://www.crf-usa.org/america-responds-to-terrorism/a-clear-and-present-danger.html

Toma, C. L., & Hancock, J. T. (2010). Looks and lies: The role of physical attractiveness in online dating self-presentation and deception. *Communication Research, 37*(3), 335–351.

Trump, D. (2017, July 1). My use of social media is not presidential—it's MODERN DAY PRESIDENTIAL. [Tweet]. Retrieved from https://twitter.com/realdonaldtrump/status/881281755017355264?lang=en

United States Courts. (n.d.). Retrieved from https://www.uscourts.gov/about-federal-courts/educational-resources/about-educational-outreach/activity-resources/what-does

United States v. O'Brien, 391 U.S. 367 (1968).

U.S. Courts.(n.d.). What Does Free Speech Mean? Retrieved from https://www.uscourts.gov/about-federal-courts/educational-resources/about-educational-outreach/activity-resources/what-does

Van Blokland, E. (2017). *Choosing the right tone in digital diplomacy* (Bachelor's thesis). Retrieved from https://openaccess.leidenuniv.nl/bitstream/handle/1887/52858/Beelaerts%20van%20Blokland-s1425439-BA%20Thesis%20IBO-2017.pdf?sequence=1

Voggeser, B. J., Singh, R. K., & Göritz, A. S. (2018). Self-control in online discussions: Disinhibited online behavior as a failure to recognize social cues. *Frontiers in Psychology, 8,* 2372.

Vosoughi, S., Roy, D., & Aral, S. (2018). The spread of true and false news online. *Science, 359*(6380), 1146–1151.

Waimberg, J. (2017, November 2). *Schenck v. United States*: Defining the limits of free speech. Retrieved from https://constitutioncenter.org/blog/schenck-v-united-states-defining-the-limits-of-free-speech/

Warner, D. E., & Raiter, M. (2005). Social context in massively-multiplayer online games (MMOGs): Ethical questions in shared space. *International Review of Information Ethics, 4*, 47–52.

Warner, D. E., & Raiter, M. (2005). Social context in massively-multiplayer online games (MMOGs): Ethical questions in shared space. *International Review of Information Ethics, 4*(7), 46–52.

Warzel, C. (2019a, March 19). We're asking the wrong questions of You-Tube and Facebook after New Zealand. *The New York Times*. Retrieved from https://www.nytimes.com/2019/03/19/opinion/facebook-you tube-new-zealand.html

Warzel, C. (2019b, March 26). Can we block a shooter's viral aspirations? *The New York Times*. Retrieved from https://www.nytimes.com/ 2019/03/26/opinion/new-zealand-shooter-video.html?action=click& module=Opinion&pgtype=Homepage

Waxman, O. B., & Fabry, M. (2018, May 4). From an anonymous tip to an impeachment: A timeline of key moments in the Clinton-Lewinsky scandal. *Time*. Retrieved from http://time.com/5120561/bill-clinton-monica-lewinsky-timeline/

Webb, L. (2015). Shame transfigured: Slut-shaming from Rome to cyberspace. *First Monday, 20*(406). Retrieved from https://firstmonday .org/ojs/index.php/fm/article/view/5464/4419

Whitty, M. T. (2008). Revealing the "real" me, searching for the "actual" you: Presentations of self on an internet dating site. *Computers in Human Behavior, 24*(4), 1707–1723.

Wittkower, D. (2014). Facebook and dramauthentic identity: A post-Goffmanian theory of identity performance on SNS. *First Monday, 19*(4). Retrieved from; https://firstmonday.org/ojs/index.php/fm/article/ view/4858/3875

Ybarra, M. L. (2004). Linkages between depressive symptomatology and Internet harassment among young regular Internet users. *Cyber-Psychology & Behavior, 7*(2), 247–257.

Ybarra, M. L., & Mitchell, K. J. (2004a). Online aggressor/targets, aggressors, and targets: A comparison of associated youth characteristics. *Journal of Child Psychology and Psychiatry, 45*(7), 1308–1316.

Ybarra, M. L., & Mitchell, K. J. (2004b). Youth engaging in online harassment: Associations with caregiver—Child relationships, internet use, and personal characteristics. *Journal of Adolescence, 27*(3), 319–336.

Yiu, Y. (2018, August 31). Battling online bots, trolls and people. *Inside Science*. Retrieved from https://www.insidescience.org/news/battling-online-bots-trolls-and-people

Zezulka, L. A., & Seigfried-Spellar, K. C. (2016). Differentiating cyberbullies and internet trolls by personality characteristics and self-esteem. *Journal of Digital Forensics, Security and Law, 11*(3), 5.

Index

Note: Page numbers followed by *f* indicate figures; page numbers followed by *n* indicate notes.

About the Author

Sheri Bauman, PhD, has worked as a licensed psychologist and a school counselor and currently is a professor in the counseling graduate program at the University of Arizona. Bauman conducts research on bullying, cyberbullying, and peer victimization, and also studies teacher responses to bullying. She is a frequent presenter on these topics at local, state, national, and international conferences. Bauman is a member of the editorial board for the *Journal of School Psychology,* and an ad-hoc reviewer for many journals, including *Aggressive Behavior, International Journal of Child-Computer Interaction, Developmental Psychology, Policing: An International Journal, Journal of School Violence,* and *New Media and Society.* She is the author, editor, coauthor, or coeditor of 7 books, and has to her credit more than 65 articles in peer-reviewed journals, 28 book chapters, and 3 training DVDs. Her books include *Cyberbullying: What Counselors Need to Know* (2011), and *Principles of Cyberbullying Research: Definitions, Measures, and Methodology* (2013), as well as *Reducing Cyberbullying in Schools: International Evidence-Based Best Practices* (2018). She is on the board of trustees of DitchtheLabel.org, an anti-bullying charity in the United Kingdom and United States, and serves as their research consultant. Her honors include the Eminent Career Award from the Association for Specialists in Group Work (ASGW), being named as an Erasmus Fellow to the College of Education at the University of Arizona, being twice chosen for the President's Distinguished Service Award from ASGW, and later for a President's Award for Extraordinary Service from the ASGW, as well as being selected for the Fulbright Specialist roster (2013–2018).